# The Importance Of Seed

Dr. C.V. White

## The Importance of Seed

Copyright @ 2015 by Dr. Cynthia V. White

All rights reserved. No part of this book may be reproduced or transmitted in any form or by any means, electronic or mechanical including photocopying, recording, or by any information storage or retrieval system, without written permission from the author.

Unless otherwise quoted all word definitions Greek and Hebrew and scripture quotations are from the King James Version of the Bible as recorded in the Blue Letter Bible: Retrieved from http://www.blueletterbible.org. All quotations from the amplified Bible were retrieved from the biblegateway.com by the Lockman Foundation.

Published by:

Dr. C.V. White formerly Fruit That Remains
150 Post Office Road Waldorf, Maryland 20604
Email: drcvwhite@gmail.com

ISBN 13: 978-1-934326-03-9
ISBN 10: 1-934326-03-8

DiViNE Purpose Publishing
www.divinepurposepublishing.com
P. O. Box 906
Branford, CT. 06405

Printed in the United States of America

## DEDICATION

This book is dedicated my biological father, Rev. Lee Andrew Townes Sr., who helped me to mature naturally and spiritually. He is the seed from which I came. My father was an inspiration to me as my father and as my pastor for many years. He started to preach when he was eight years old and continued for seventy-two years. For fifty of those years, he pastored churches and during that time he was instrumental in the spiritual growth of many aspiring pastors and clergy. I would also like to thank Bishop Rodney S. Walker I, my spiritual father, who has been instrumental in my spiritual growth. Bishop Walker, I appreciate your support while I was attending school, working, and preparing for ministry. You have been and still are a great blessing to me! Every step of the way you encouraged me to continue with my writing projects. I am appreciative of all of your efforts to assist me in this project and in other areas of my life. I also appreciate God for giving me such a wonderful spiritual father in you! You are a special gift from God and I will always cherish everything that you have poured into me all of these years.

I want to thank my mother, Cynthia Ollie Mary Townes Turner, for giving birth to me and helping me in every way she possible could. I also would like to thank my children, Myrna White, Gregory T. White Jr., Lance White, Larry White, Laura White and Demise.

## APPRECIATION

I would like to take this opportunity to thank Bishop Rodney S. Walker I, Paulette Walker, Lisa Burgess and Divine Purpose Publishing for their support and assistance in the preparation of this book for publication.

I appreciate your willingness to meet the challenges necessary to complete the final preparation for printing and distribution. Your ideas and suggestions contributed immensely to the success of this project. It was so good to have you as part of the team. I am confident that good things will come from our joint efforts. Thank you again, for a job well done!

## Table of Contents

Introduction ............................................................. 6

Chapter 1 The Holy Seed of God/
The Unholy Seed of Adam ................................... 17

Chapter 2 The WORD of God Is Seed ................. 26

Chapter 3 Different Kind of Seed ........................ 35

Chapter 4 Christ "The Seed" In Jesus ................. 48

Chapter 5 The Seed of Abraham .......................... 61

Chapter 6 The Seed of David (The King) ........... 74

Chapter 7 Jesus The Son of Man – (Natural and Spiritual) Seed ................................................................. 82

Chapter 8 The Seed of Jesus Christ .................... 102

Chapter 9 The Seed of the New Testament ....... 113

Chapter 10 The Seed of the Covenant ................ 135

# INTRODUCTION

Seed is something that we take for granted. We don't think much about it even though we are aware of the purpose of it and how it operates. Seed is so important that we can't get anything accomplished without it. Everything we do is seed, everything we say is seed and everything we think is seed. Behaviors and habits are seed; good and bad deeds are seed. Nothing can be accomplished without seed. If we can't accomplish anything without it, why are we not more aware of our situations in the natural and in the spirit?

We are not aware because we have not paid attention to what happens in the natural with seed. God mentions it in the beginning, but we have to be aware of what seed is in the spirit and then look at the operation of seed in the natural in order to understand why we can't do anything without seed.

The purpose of this study is to identify the importance of seed and use it correctly in the spirit and in the natural. Let's start by taking a look at what happened in the beginning. When we read Genesis Chapter 1, we notice something that God did repeatedly to bring things into existence.

In Genesis 1:1, we see that in the beginning that God created the heaven and the earth. The Hebrew word for God in this passage is 'elohiym, a masculine noun that means (plural) the plurality of God, the Father, the Son, and the Holy Spirit. All three are working together to make this happen. And in verse 2, we see that the situation of the earth was bleak to say the least, but notice what happened. God the Father thought about the situation.

***Genesis 1:2 And the earth was without form, and void; and darkness [was] upon the face of the deep. And the Spirit of God moved upon the face of the waters.***

The Holy Spirit moved upon the face of the waters and with the wisdom of God they begin to correct the situation. Notice also that the Son spoke and then situation changed. We see that God spoke in Genesis 1:3.

***Genesis 1:3 And God said, Let there be light: and there was light.***

After God the Father thought it, God the Son said, and God the Holy Spirit did what was said. Now we get the process work- ing together, God the Father thought about the wisdom of what to do, God the Son spoke (said) that thought and God the Holy Spirit made it happen. All of this was done simultaneously in the spirit realm to bring manifestation in the natural realm. This process was repeated over and over again until the work was finished. Let's look at a few more examples.

Genesis 1:6 - And ***God said***, Let there be a firmament in the midst of the waters, and let it divide the waters from the waters.

Genesis 1:9 - And God said, Let the waters under the heaven be gathered together unto one place, and let the dry [land] appear: and it was so.

Genesis1:14 - And ***God said***, Let there be lights in the firmament of the heaven to divide the day from the night; and let them be for signs, and for seasons, and for days, and years:

Genesis 1:26 - And **God said**, Let us make man in our image, after our likeness: and let them have dominion over the fish of the sea, and over the fowl of the air, and over the cattle, and over all the earth, and over every creeping thing that creepeth upon the earth.

Genesis 1:28 And God blessed them, and **God said** unto them, Be fruitful, and multi- ply, and replenish the earth, and subdue it: and have dominion over the fish of the sea, and over the fowl of the air, and over every living thing that moveth upon the earth.

Now the Hebrew word for <u>said</u> in these passages is 'amar, it is a verb (an action word) that means 1) to say, speak, utter, to say, to answer, to say in one's heart, to think. Remember we are still talking about seed. Now to clarify that nothing was done or can be done without seed, let's find out where God explained that His Word is seed. We find that in Luke 8:11.

*Luke 8:11 Now the parable is this: The seed is the word of God.*

We also know that the Word of God is synonymous with the Son of God. We can see that in John when he was talking Jesus Christ. The book of John presents Jesus Christ God. He starts the book by talking about Jesus Christ being the word of God. Let's look at this in John 1:1-3.

*John 1:1-3 1 In the beginning was the Word, and the Word was with God, and the Word was God. 2 The same was in the beginning with God*

*3 All things were made by him; and without him was not any thing made that was made.*

From this passage, notice that the Word in the Greek is logos that is a masculine noun (Jesus Christ) which means: 1) of speech a) a word, uttered by a living voice, embodies a conception or idea b) what someone has said 1) a word 2) the sayings of God 3) decree, mandate or order 4) of the moral precepts given by God 5) Old Testament prophecy given by the prophets 6) what is declared, a thought, declaration, aphorism, a weighty saying.

There is more but this is sufficient to get an understanding of Jesus Christ being the word of God. Now this passage also states that the word was with God in the beginning, as we have seen in Genesis that the Word is God. It is further stated by the Father Himself that Jesus Christ is His Son to Peter while they were on the mount of transfiguration in Matthew 17:4-5.

*Matthew 17:4-5 Then answered Peter, and said unto Jesus, Lord, it is good for us to be here: if thou wilt, let us make here three tabernacles; one for thee, and one for Moses, and one for Elias. 5 While he yet spake, behold, a bright cloud over- shadowed them: and behold a voice out of the cloud, which said, This is my beloved Son, in whom I am well pleased; hear ye him.*

Now that we can see how the Seed operated in the Beginning, we can now follow God wisdom through the Bible to see how to apply it to our lives and have it produce for us in this day and time. As we finish this study, it will become clear to us and we can begin to plant and sow seed to receive the harvest we desire. We will talk more about the Word of God being seed later in this study.

God is a good God and everything that He created is good and has a good purpose. Seed is very interesting and important in that it was mentioned specifically as to how it functions as a part of the reproduction process. As we go through this study, we will find out about the purpose and plan of God for the seed.

In the natural, a seed is a "vessel" which contains, protects and aids in distribution of the embryo (zygote) of the plant or tree to a new destination. And inside the seed, you will find that a typical seed includes three basic parts: (1) an embryo, (2) a supply of nutrients for the embryo, and (3) a seed coat. Some seeds are protected by its fruit. That sounds wonderful – your seed is protected by your fruit. Let's find out what all of this means in this study.

> ***Genesis 1:11-12 And God said, Let the earth bring forth grass, the herb yielding seed, [and] the fruit tree yielding fruit after his kind, whose seed [is] in itself, upon the earth: and it was so. 12 And the earth brought forth grass, [and] herb yielding seed after his kind, and the tree yielding fruit, whose seed [was] in itself, after his kind: and God saw that [it was] good.***

We see here that God commanded the earth, *a feminine noun* in Hebrew, to bring forth some things; however, God provided the initial seed, *the masculine noun*. The earth was commanded to bring forth grass and herb yielding seed and the tree yielding fruit of whose seed was in itself after his kind. Notice here that God described the seed as male and that the seed in itself after his kind and then God said that was good.

The Hebrew word for seed is *zera*` a masculine noun which means **1) seed, sowing, offspring a) a sowing b) seed c) semen virile d) offspring, descendants, posterity, children e) of moral quality 1) a practitioner of righteousness (fig.) f) sowing time (by meton).** The grass and herb yields seed, but the tree's seed is in its fruit. The Hebrew word for "after his kind" is "miyn" a masculine noun pronounced men that means **kind**, sometimes a species (usually of animals)/Groups of living organisms belong in the same created "kind" if they have descended from the same ancestral gene pool. The Hebrew word for *fruit* is *pĕriy* which means **a) fruit, produce (of the ground), b) fruit, offspring, children, progeny (of the womb), c) fruit (of actions) (fig.).**

### God's Seed

After God explained about the seed He created man, His own *seed*. God formed man out of the same earth (dust) that He commanded to bring forth the living things (seed) and breathed His own **Spiritual DNA** (deoxyribonucleic acid, a self-replicating material, symbolic of the holy seed) into man. Now man has God's given ability to grow things in the spirit as the earth has to grow things in the natural.

> *Genesis 2:7 And the LORD God formed man [of] the dust of the ground, and breathed into his nostrils the breath of life; and man became a living soul.*

God blessed them, gave them their assignment and then told that what they were to eat in the natural. All of this is mentioned in Genesis 1:27-29.

> *Genesis 1:27-29 So God created man in his [own] image, in the image of God created he him; male and female created he them.*

Gender does not matter in this instance because God called man him, male and female God created them in a "him". The Hebrew word for man is *'adam* a masculine noun which means 1) man, mankind a) man, human being b) man, mankind (much more frequently intended sense in OT) c) Adam, first man this is confirmed in Genesis 5:2.

> *Genesis 5:2 Male and female created he them; and blessed them, and called their name Adam, in the day when they were created.*

God called them both Adam. Then God in verse 28 blessed him, gave him an assignment and told them what to eat.

> *Genesis 1:28-29 And God blessed them, and God said unto them, Be fruitful, and multiply, and replenish the earth, and subdue it: and have dominion over the fish of the sea, and over the fowl of the air, and over every living thing that moveth upon the earth. 29 And God said, Behold, I have given you every herb bearing seed, which [is] upon the face of all the earth, and every tree, in the which [is] the fruit of a tree yielding seed; to you it shall be for meat.*

# THE IMPORTANCE OF SEED

God mentions the natural food of herb bearing seed and every tree with fruit yielding seed for man, but to the beast of the earth, fowl of the air and everything that crept upon the earth that has life He gave only the green herb to eat.

*Genesis 1:30 And to every beast of the earth, and to every fowl of the air, and to every thing that creepeth upon the earth, wherein [there is] life, [I have given] every green herb for meat: and it was so.*

There were also in the mist of the Garden two other very important trees, the tree of life and the tree of the knowledge of good and evil. The tree of were used to nourish the eternal state of the physical body and the spiritual DNA. The spiritual food for Adam would be the Word of God. God spoke with Adam and as long as he obeyed the word of God he would be feeding his spiritual man well and was able to grow spiritual things only.

God allowed Adam to eat from every tree, including the tree of life and as long as he obeyed God he would have no problems freeing his spirit man good spiritual food.

*Genesis 2:9 And out of the ground made the LORD God to grow every tree that is pleasant to the sight, and good for food; the tree of life also in the midst of the garden, and the tree of knowledge of good and evil.*

The tree of life was a tree that was going to allow him to live forever as long as he continued to eat from it. God mentioned this in Genesis 3:22.

*Genesis 3:22 - And the LORD God said, Behold, the man is become as one of us, to know good and evil: and now, lest he put forth his hand, and take also of the tree of life, and eat, and live for ever:*

They were clear on natural food, they needed natural food for the natural body, but they also needed spiritual food to feed the life that God had breathed into them. The physical body is just a shell and it will do whatever it is told to do. If led by your spirit man it will follow and if led by the natural man it will follow. Therefore, we have to feed the spiritual man with more spiritual food (seed) than we feed the natural man with natural food (seed) so that our spirit man can gain control and led our natural physical body by our spirit and not position our natural physical body to be led by our flesh.

**Natural Seed**

In order to understand from this point you have to understand how the seeds work in the agriculture process. Seed is the reproductive instrument of flowering plants, not all plants produce seed, therefore it is important for us to understand why God mentions seed plants specifically. First let us examine the seed. Seeds are made up of an embryo plant and the food source to feed it until it becomes large enough to feed itself through the photosynthesis process.

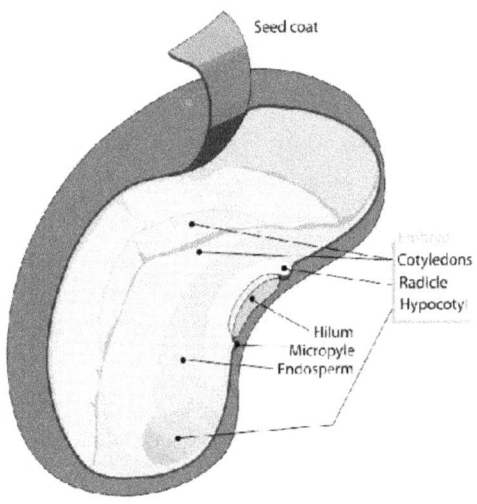

The seed structure: The embryo contains:

>Cotyledons – an embryonic leaf part of the embryo
Radicle - the part of a plant embryo that develops into the primary root
Hypocotyl - the stem part of an embryo plant

The food source: Endosperm is food for the developing plant.

Hilum - the mark showing where the seed was formally attached to the plant

Micropyle - the opening in the ovule of through which the pollen tube enters

Once the seed is planted in the earth (soil) it begins to grow. Notice that everything that the seed needs to reproduce is in it already and everything that the soil needs to grow the seed is already in it. Also notice that the seed and the soil are both portable. You can move them both to other locations and they will still produce as long as the climate and the atmosphere are conducive to that particular species.

There is another Hebrew word that is closely related to seed that word is sow "zara" this is a verb, an action word meaning) to sow, scatter seed

a) (Qal) - 1) to sow, 2) producing, yielding seed
b) (Niphal) - 1) to be sown, 2) to become pregnant, be made pregnant
c) (Pual) to be sown
d) (Hiphil) to produce seed, yield seed

The seed does not produce unless it is sown. If you do not plant it into the earth or ground in the natural or in the spirit, you will not get a harvest from that particular seed. Therefore as we continue this study let us remember that the seed needs to be planted or sown, so that the earth (spiritual or natural) will bring forth the seeds reproducing after its own kind.

# CHAPTER 1

# The Holy Seed of God/ The Unholy Seed of Adam

After God created the original (first seed bearing), plant, animal, fish, bird or man the seed continues to reproduce after its own kind. This simple natural process explains a powerful spiritual principle of growing spiritual seed. In the natural you can choose what seeds to plant and so it is in the spirit, you can choose. God gave Adam the correct start so that he would get the crop that he desired but he did have a choice of choosing God's crop or another.

Now let us take a look at the instructions that God gave to Adam (male and female), remember they were both in Adam, which would cause His spiritual DNA to cease to exist. In order to remain God's seed with God's DNA Adam would have to be obedient to God's instructions were very important because Adam would have to choose to keep God's DNA or exchange it for anther. God's DNA inside the seed reproduced life, however, it is possible for the DNA inside the seed to produce death. God warned Adam about this in Genesis 2:17.

> *Genesis 2:17 - But of the tree of the knowledge of good and evil, thou shalt not eat of it: for in the day that thou eatest thereof thou shalt surely die.*

Once Adam (remember, God called them both Adam) ate from the tree of the knowledge of good and evil God spoke to them again and let them know that Adam, God seed (son) no longer carried the holy seed, because he had exchanged it for an unholy seed and now he is going to reproduce unholy seed from this point on. God spoke to the serpent, representing Satan first Genesis 3:15.

> *Genesis 3:15 - And I will put enmity between thee and the woman, and between thy seed and her seed; it shall bruise thy head, and thou shalt bruise his heel.*

God is talking about seed again. The seed is the male and the woman is the earth bringing forth the seed. She is the one that will bring forth the seed. She understands that principle as she expounds on her new seed when Abel was killed by his broth- er. They were both her seed but once her son Abel, who carried the holy seed was killed by his brother Cain, his brother was exiled and she needed another male (seed) that would carry the holy seed. She called him Seth in Genesis 4:25.

> *Genesis 4:25 - And Adam knew his wife again; and she bare a son, and called his name Seth: For God, [said she], hath appointed me another seed instead of Abel, whom Cain slew.*

Now remember that seed has the embro inside and all of the genetics to reproduce after its own kind. Seth would be the beginning of the ancestry line of the holy seed. Then God spoke to the woman in Genesis 3:16.

> *Genesis 3:16 - unto the woman he said, I will greatly multiply thy sorrow and thy conception; in sorrow thou shalt bring forth children; and*

***thy desire [shall be] to thy husband, and he shall rule over thee.***

At this point God is calling her woman, the man with the womb because He is talking to her about conception (receiving seed) and bringing forth children (reproducing seed). This is the first time that God spoke to them individually as He talked with them and the serpent in response Adam (male and female) eating the forbidden fruit of the tree of the knowledge of good and evil. First God spoke to the serpent (Satan) about the fate of his seed and then to the woman about the coming of her seed and the fact that her assignment will be bringing forth the seed of the man and finally to Adam himself about the damage of his seed.

Now the earth has to be plowed and broken up in order to do what it needs to do. And to the man God said Genesis 3:17,

***Genesis 3:17 - And unto Adam he said, Because thou hast hearkened unto the voice of thy wife, and hast eaten of the tree, of which I commanded thee, saying, Thou shalt not eat of it: cursed [is] the ground for thy sake; in sorrow shalt thou eat [of] it all the days of thy life.***

Now Adam, the seed of God you have changed your holy seed to an unholy seed, you have caused your wife, the ground (earth) to bring forth in sorrow and you will eat of that spiritual food all the days of your life. God also changed the natural food that Adam would eat, the way he would get the food and removed his eternal status.

> *Genesis 3:18 Thorns also and thistles shall it bring forth to thee; and thou shalt eat the herb of the field;*
>
> *Genesis 3:19 In the sweat of thy face shalt thou eat bread, till thou return unto the ground; for out of it wast thou taken: for dust thou [art], and unto dust shalt thou return.*

Unholy seed cannot have eternal status in the presence of God, only holy seed can have that kind of status. They have to eat bread now naturally and spiritually. God would have to send another seed to redeem and restore to her (the womb Adam, woman) a holy seed but for now Adam (mankind) would have to wait for another holy seed. Jesus explained why the spirit needed to feed on the word of God in Matthew 4:4.

> *Matthew 4:4 - But he answered and said, It is writ- ten, Man shall not live by bread alone, but by every word that proceedeth out of the mouth of God.*

### Protection and Preservation of the Holy Seed

God is preserving the holy seed down through the generations until it is time to keep the word that he gave to the serpent. The Messiah and Redeemer will be born and He is the seed of the woman.

Now God has given us the understanding that He is going to protect and preserve His holy seed until the woman (earth) yields it and brings it forth. He talks to Noah about this after He destroyed the earth with a flood and started all over with Noah and his family. God finished his conversations with Noah by explaining the permanent position and importance of seedtime and harvest in Genesis 8:22.

*Genesis 8:22 - While the earth remaineth, seedtime and harvest, and cold and heat, and summer and winter, and day and night shall not cease.*

God is saying in this passage that as long as the earth remains there is always going to be seedtime (this word is Zera the same as seed explained earlier) and harvest, the Hebrew word for harvest is qatsiyr, a masculine noun that means 1) harvest, harvesting a) process of harvesting b) crop, what is harvested or reaped c) time of harvest 2) boughs, branches. Therefore, we are not going to be able to operate without seedtime and harvest and in addition, there will always be seasons of harvest in the hot summer seasons and the cold fall and winter seasons.

The Hebrew word for summer is qayits, a masculine noun meaning 1) summer, summer-fruit and winter is choreph, a masculine noun meaning harvest time, autumn, winter. And these will be governed by day and night. Day in this passage is yowm, a masculine noun meaning 1) day, time, year a) day (as opposed to night), b) day (24 hour period), 1) as defined by evening and morning in Genesis 1, 2) as a division of time, a) a working day, a day's journey, c) days, lifetime (pl.), d) time, period (general), e) year, f) temporal references, 1) today, 2) yesterday.

The Hebrew word for night is layil, masculine noun layil meaning 1) night a) night (as opposed to day), b) of gloom, protective shadow (fig.). The end of this verse says plainly that this process will never cease. Shall not cease in the Hebrew shabath and it means 1) to cease, desist, rest, a) (Qal), 1) to cease, 2) to rest, desist (from labour), b) (Niphal) to cease, c) (Hiphil). 1) to cause to cease, put an end to, 2) to exterminate, destroy, 3) to cause to desist from, 4) to remove, 5) to cause to fail, 2) (Qal) to keep or observe the Sabbath. All of this is not going to happen to seedtime and harvest nor will the seasons of harvest stop as long as the earth remains. God shared this after Noah gave his burnt offerings to the Lord.

When God destroyed the earth by flood, He saved the seed through Noah. He was concerned about keeping seed alive and He articulated that to Noah. So He prepared Noah for the flood and He told Noah what to do in order to preserve the seed in Genesis 7:1-3.

*Genesis 7:1-3 1 And the LORD said unto Noah, Come thou and all thy house into the ark; for thee have I seen righteous before me in this generation. 2 Of every clean beast thou shalt take to thee by sevens, the male and his female: and of beasts that [are] not clean by two, the male and his female. 3 Of fowls also of the air by sevens, the male and the female; to keep seed alive upon the face of all the earth.*

God made a covenant with Noah and part of that covenant was about his seed, his sons seed, and the seed of all of the living creatures that came out the ark with him.

*Genesis 9:8-11 And God spake unto Noah, and to his sons with him, saying, 9 And I, behold, I establish my covenant with you, and with your seed after you; Gen 10 And with every living creature that [is] with you, of the fowl, of the cattle, and of every beast of the earth with you; from all that go out of the ark, to every beast of the earth. 11 And I will establish my covenant with you; neither shall all flesh be cut off any more by the waters of a flood; neither shall there any more be a flood to destroy the earth.*

God continued to watch over the holy seed until He established a father to bring the seed trough. That father was Abram; later know as Abraham, the name God gave him.

*Genesis 12:7 And the LORD appeared unto Abram, and said, Unto thy seed will I give this land: and there builded he an altar unto the LORD, who appeared unto him.*

God's conversations with Abraham were about the covenant that He would give him and his seed:

1. God promised him land for his seed.

    Genesis 12:7 And the LORD appeared unto Abram, and said, Unto thy seed will I give this land: and there builded he an altar unto the LORD, who appeared unto him.

    Genesis 13:15 For all the land which thou seest, to thee will I give it, and to thy seed for ever.

2. God promised seed that he could not count.

    Genesis 13:16 And I will make thy seed as the dust of the earth: so that if a man can number the dust of the earth, [then] shall thy seed also be numbered.

Genesis 15:5 And he brought him forth abroad, and said, Look now toward heaven, and tell the stars, if thou be able to number them: and he said unto him, So shall thy seed be.

Genesis 15:13 And he said unto Abram, Know of a surety that thy seed shall be a stranger in a land [that is] not theirs, and shall serve them; and they shall afflict them four hundred years;

Genesis 15:18 In the same day the LORD made a covenant with Abram, saying, Unto thy seed have I given this land, from the river of Egypt unto the great river, the river Euphrates:

Genesis 17:7 And I will establish my covenant between me and thee and thy seed after thee in their generations for an ever- lasting covenant, to be a God unto thee, and to thy seed after thee.

Genesis 17:8 And I will give unto thee, and to thy seed after thee, the land wherein thou art a stranger, all the land of Canaan, for an everlasting possession; and I will be their God.

Genesis 17:9 And God said unto Abraham, Thou shalt keep my covenant therefore, thou, and thy seed after thee in their generations.

Genesis 17:10 This [is] my covenant, which ye shall keep, between me and you and thy seed after thee; Every man child among you shall be circumcised. Gen 17:12 And he that is eight days old shall be circumcised among you, every man child in your generations, he that is born in the house, or bought with money of any stranger, which [is] not of thy seed.

Abraham was the carrier of the seed but he could not bring the seed forth, he needed his wife (the earth) to bring the seed forth. God spoke to Abraham and told him who to send the seed through, Sarah, his wife in Genesis 17:19.

***Genesis 17:19 And God said, Sarah thy wife shall bear thee a son indeed; and thou shalt call his name Isaac: and I will establish my covenant with him for an everlasting covenant, [and] with his seed after him.***

Abraham being the seed carrier can choose to bring it forth through any female that he chooses but God was very clear to him of who should bring forth the holy seed. Abraham did bring forth his seed through 2 other women and their children call him father also so in the natural they can produce what seed produces but in the spirit only the one designed to carry the holy seed can do so.

## *CHAPTER 2*

## The WORD of God Is Seed

Notice from this point on of how God stays in touch with that seed that He spoke to the Serpent about in Genesis 3:15 from that time until now. God is still taking about seed. Jesus spoke to us about seed and the importance of our understanding one of the divine natures of the Kingdom of Heaven with a parable about sowing seed and the results of sowing of bad ground or good ground. The seed that Jesus spoke to us about was the word of God. We are the ground, and we are also the sowers. We must sow the Word of God as explained in Mark 4:14. The sower soweth the word. The Word is seed.

> *Luke 8:11 Now the parable is this: The seed is the word of God.*

Notice that Jesus talks about the ground (earth) receiving the seed. We can receive it on good ground and it will be multiplied according to our faith. The seed sowed in the good ground is mentioned in Matthew 13:23.

> *But he that received seed into the good ground is he that heareth the word, and understandeth [it]; which also beareth fruit, and bringeth forth, some an hundredfold, some sixty, some thirty.*

However, good seed can be sown in the field. The field is the world and while you are sleeping your enemy can sow some bad seed in your field. When we wake up and see the bad croup growing with our good crop, our first reaction would be to pull of the bad plants. But Jesus said that we should not do that immediately and that we should wait until harvest time to separate so that we will not lose any of the good seeds.

This is very interesting, because now we cannot give up on people just because they have made some bad choices or just have not grown up or for whatever reason we cannot reject them. Giving them a chance to grow with the good plants gives them opportunity to see a better way, the possibility of doing things another way, other options, to experience love and understanding that they may have never seen before.

God would have spared Sodom and Gomorrah if there had just been ten righteous people in the city. There were not ten there but the entire city of evil and sinful people could have been spared because of ten. Abraham was asking for the life of the people that God had decided to destroy because of their evil, but Abraham asked God to spare them for the sake of a small number of righteous. He started asking for 50 but eventually got down to 10 and God would have saved Sodom for 10. Take a look at that in Genesis 18:22-24.

***Genesis 18:22-24 And the men turned their faces from thence, and went toward Sodom: but Abraham stood yet before the LORD. 23 And Abraham drew near, and said, Wilt thou also destroy the righteous with the wicked? 24 peradventure there be fifty righteous within the city: wilt thou also destroy and not spare the place for the fifty righteous that [are] therein?***

And finally God said I will not destroy it for 10's sake.

*Genesis 18:32 And he said, Oh let not the Lord be angry, and I will speak yet but this once: Peradventure ten shall be found there. And he said, I will not destroy [it] for ten's sake.*

Jesus gives us example about this with His mention of the Kingdom of Heaven with this parable.

*Matthew 13:24-30 Another parable put he forth unto them, saying, The kingdom of heaven is likened unto a man which sowed good seed in his field: 25 But while men slept, his enemy came and sowed tares among the wheat, and went his way. 26 But when the blade was sprung up, and brought forth fruit, then appeared the tares also. 27 So the servants of the householder came and said unto him, Sir, didst not thou sow good seed in thy field? From whence then hath it tares? 28 He said unto them, An enemy hath done this. The servants said unto him, Wilt thou then that we go and gather them up? 29 But he said, Nay; lest while ye gather up the tares, ye root up also the wheat with them. 30 Let both grow together until the harvest: and in the time of harvest I will say to the reapers, Gather ye together first the tares, and bind them in bundles to burn them: but gather the wheat into my barn.*

Now let us not forget the possibility of receiving bad seed in our ground. Many times we blame God for some things that He has nothing to do with. If we do not prepare our ground by way of process we will not necessarily be good ground to receive the seed (word of God). We cannot care more about the cares of this world, riches, people's opinions, etc., we cannot be led by our emotions and be shut down because of afflictions or persecutions etc., because these things will hinder the process of us becoming good ground. God sent us Jesus Christ (His Word) and He is a good seed, however we must prepare our ground to receive the word of God. See by this scripture what happens if we are not good ground.

*Mark 4:13-19 And he said unto them, Know ye not this parable? and how then will ye know all parables? 14 <u>The sower soweth the word</u>. 15 And these are they by the way side, where the word is sown; but when they have heard, Satan cometh immediately, and taketh away the word that was sown in their hearts. 16 And these are they likewise which are sown on stony ground; who, when they have heard the word, immediately receive it with glad- ness; 17 And have no root in themselves, and so endure but for a time: afterward, when affliction or persecution ariseth for the word's sake, immediately they are offended. 18 And these are they which are sown among thorns; such as hear the word, 19 And the cares of this world, and the deceitfulness of riches, and the lusts of other things entering in, choke the word, and it becometh unfruitful.*

Notice how important this parable about seed and sowing is because Jesus explains that you can understand all parables if you understand this one "the parable of the sower."

God continues to keep the discussion of seed in the hearts and minds of the people especially those that carry the Holy Seed. He mentions to Isaac and Jacob the seed that he promised their father and grandfather Abraham. The one seed that continues to be brought forth to the forefront is that one seed that will save the world, the seed of Abraham.

As much as we want to only think about seed being only good and lovely we do have to confront the fact that we can create seed in the spirit by our words, actions and deeds. God said something in Genesis that is fascinating to me. I am sure most people don't think too much about this but I think that it is great. God said something to Noah when he came out of the Ark, released all the animal and gave an offering unto the Lord that should cause us never to continue to be angry with anybody ever again but to pray for them for they know not what they do. God said to Noah in His concern about what happened to the earth and its inhabitants because of the flood in Genesis 8:21-22.

*Genesis 8:21-22 And the LORD smelled a sweet savour; and the LORD said in his heart, I will not again curse the ground any more for man's sake; for the imagination of man's heart [is] evil from his youth; neither will I again smite any more every thing living, as I have done. 22 While the earth remaineth, seedtime and harvest, and cold and heat, and summer and winter, and day and night shall not cease.*

God is explaining to Noah a natural law that He was putting in place for the physical earth about seed. God said that while the earth remains that He will not destroy (curse) the earth for man's sake. He will not flood the earth again, so there will always be seedtime and harvest. But remember we also have a spiritual seed and it is going to be whatever we say, do or think is some cases. So whatever people do will be done to them because they planted the seed and they are going to get a harvest of that type of seed.

This law cannot be changed for our convenience; we will have what we say over ourselves or over other people. We will get the harvest of our seed even if it is does not seem good to us. For instance ever kind of seed reproduces after its own kind, so if you sow (plant) love you will get a harvest of love; if you sow meanness you will get a harvest of meanness. It is a trick of the Devil for us to think that we can plant one kind of seed and get another kind of crop and harvest time. That is why it is very important that we pray for one another because most of us do not know the agri- culture process of planting and receiving a harvest and as a result most people don't even know that they are getting the harvest of the seeds that they planted.

**Multiplied Seed**

God uses the agriculture system to explain how all of this operates. You can never get only one seed back when you plant just one. For instance, if you plant an apple tree, it takes only one seed. You get an apple tree from that one seed, you can count the seeds in one apple but you cannot count the apples in one seed. If you plant one peanut seed, you get a peanut plant. The peanut plant produces peanut as a part of a root system. They are all under the ground, but when you pull up the plant from the ground it will have sometimes over 100 peanuts attached to that one plant. So you can count the peanuts in one shell but you cannot count the peanuts in one seed.

This process will continue generation after generation and that is why you cannot count them. I said all that about seed naturally to say this about spiritual seed, if you plant one act of grief in someone life how much more is your harvest going to be in the return of the grief that you can expect, wow, we need to seriously pray for people instead of getting angry with them for they know not the harvest of the thing. God is in the multiplication business and when we obey Him we get a great harvest from that seed.

What is God up to? After all of this He is still talking about seed. God gives us seed in the natural and he protects our seed even when we don't realized that it needs protection. God is leading us to one seed, but the process has to be in spiritual order and at the time God has determined for it to be and when we get the revelation of God's divine plan concerning our seed we would rest easy and not be so concerned about what God has for us.

What God has promised in His word is truth. He will not let us be without seed, but we must trust God in this. He gives us many examples in His word about His faithfulness in this very thing. Remember, Judah, Jacobs's son? His story is fascinating in regard to his seed. Judah had 3 sons. Two of his sons died because of the evil deeds that they did. That left Judah with only one son and he did not want to lose that son so he did not obey the spiritual law in regards to him giving his last son to the widow of his first son, Tamar, so that his first son's seed would continue in the earth.

***Genesis 38:6 And Judah took a wife for Er his firstborn, whose name [was] Tamar.***

When Judah second son dies he told Tamar to remain a widow and wait for his third son was ready.

## THE IMPORTANCE OF SEED

*Genesis 38:13 And it was told Tamar, saying, Behold thy father in law goeth up to Timnath to shear his sheep.*

*Genesis 38:11 Then said Judah to Tamar his daughter in law, Remain a widow at thy father's house, till Shelah my son be grown: for he said, Lest peradventure he die also, as his brethren [did]. And Tamar went and dwelt in her father's house.*

Then some time after Judah's wife died he planned a trip to shear his sheep and Tamar heard about this trip. She knew that Judah's son was now of age to marry but Judah did not offer him to be her husband The account of this can be found in Genesis 38:11.

Remember that Judah had three sons, two are now dead and he only has one left. Tamar went to Timnath and pretended to be a harlot and Judah took advantage of her services. As a result, she became pregnant by Judah with two sons. Judah wanted to destroy her when he found out that she was pregnant but he did not give her his last son for fear of his death. He was very severe with her for wrong doing but did not consider what he had done, nevertheless God was bless- ing both of them and neither of them understood the importance of their seed.

What Judah wanted to do to Tamar when he found out she was pregnant is found in Genesis 38:24.

*Genesis 38:24 And it came to pass about three months after, that it was told Judah, saying, Tamar thy daughter in law hath played the harlot; and also, behold, she [is] with child by whoredom. And Judah said, Bring her forth, and let her be burnt.*

But when he found out that he was the father he said that she was more righteous than he. She was about to replace the two sons that he had lost and one of her sons, Pharez would be the holy seed in his generation. Judah now has three sons again. God not only did not let him be without three sons but would use one of his sons to pass the holy seed through to the next generation. God provided seed for Judah and for Tamar.

## CHAPTER 3
## Different Kind of Seed Peculiar Seed

It is very important that we understand how important seed is to God and that He is no respect of persons and His love transcends time. Remember, we talked about Abraham's seed earlier, but now let's talk about the seed of a person that Abraham loved his nephew "Lot". God did not forget Lot and made a special point to include his seed in the lineage of the holy seed.

This was indeed a peculiar situation because many generations later as we trace the seed of Judah and Tamar we find that God selected Ruth a decedent of Lot, she was a Moabite, the great-grandmother of King David. Her story is most peculiar because of how her people came about. We would never believe that God would choose such persons be a part of preserving His holy seed.

During the time of the destruction of Sodom and Gomorrah, Lot and his family were led out of the city in order to save their lives. In the process, Lot lost his wife when she looked back and became a pillar of salt. In addition, his two daughters' husbands did not believe Lot when he told them that the city was going to be destroyed and they both refused to leave with Lot, his wife and his two daughters. Because of fear they eventually ended up living in caves for a time and during that time his daughters deliberately planned to get him drunk and commit incest with him so that they could become pregnant and preserved his seed.

As a result, both daughters became pregnant. The older daughter's son Moab is the one that Ruth is a descendent of and it seems after what they did that they would never be a candidate to be the lineage of the holy seed. Even now people are discussing why God saved them for Sodom if He knew they were going to practice incest. This is amazing because it was said of Ruth by the people in the city where she lived that her seed Pharez, the son of Judah and Taman. We see that in Ruth 4:12.

> *Ruth 4:12 And let thy house be like the house of Pharez, whom Tamar bare unto Judah, of the seed which the LORD shall give thee of this young woman. KJV*

What is even more peculiar is the relationship that caused Ruth to be positioned to be in the lineage of the holy seed and that was the family of her mother-in-law Naomi. Here is a woman who had lost all of her seed but God not only restored seed to her but also to her daughter-in-law Ruth. Naomi lost her husband and her sons. There was not seed left for her. Her sons were married but neither one has any children. The account of this story is found in Ruth 1:1-16.

> *Ruth 1:1-5 In the days when the judges ruled,[a] there was a famine in the land. So a man from Bethlehem in Judah, together with his wife and two sons, went to live for a while in the country of Moab. 2 The man's name was Elimelek, his wife's name was Naomi, and the names of his two sons were Mahlon and Kilion. They were Ephrathites from Bethlehem, Judah. And they*

***went to Moab and lived there. 3 Now Elimelek, Naomi's husband, died, and she was left with her two sons. 4 They married Moabite women, one named Orpah and the other Ruth. After they had lived there about ten years, 5 both Mahlon and Kilion also died, and Naomi was left without her two sons and her husband. NIV***

It seemed to Naomi that all hope was lost and that God had given her a raw deal and that is what Judah thought when his sons died. He no longer trusted God to replenish his seed. Naomi decided to return to Bethlehem. She did not think that God would replenish her seed so she instructed her daughters-in-law to return to their families and she would return to Bethlehem to get food and shelter.

God had provided seed for all three women but Orpah decided not to trust the God of Naomi and return to her people. She missed an opportunity to live with the people of God because there were two men in Bethlehem that would have had to fulfill their duties as a kinsman redeemer (a kinsman redeemer is the relative who restores or preserves the full community rights of disadvantaged family members) to the two widow women. Naomi had land that her kinsmen could redeem for her. The land also belonged to her sons and therefore their widows.

The Book of Ruth chapter 1 tells this story better than I can; notice what happened in Ruth 1:6-18.

***Ruth 1:6-18 When Naomi heard in Moab that the Lord had come to the aid of his people by providing food for them, she and her daughters-in-law pre- pared to return home from there. 7***

*With her two daughters-in-law she left the place where she had been living and set out on the road that would take them back to the land of Judah. 8 Then Naomi said to her two daughters-in-law, "Go back, each of you, to your mother's home. May the Lord show you kindness, as you have shown kindness to your dead husbands and to me. 9 May the Lord grant that each of you will find rest in the home of another husband." Then she kissed them goodbye and they wept aloud 10 and said to her, "We will go back with you to your people." 11 But Naomi said, "Return home, my daughters. Why would you come with me? Am I going to have any more sons, who could become your husbands? 12 Return home, my daughters; I am too old to have another husband. Even if I thought there was still hope for me—even if I had a husband tonight and then gave birth to sons— 13 would you wait until they grew up? Would you remain unmarried for them? No, my daughters. It is more bitter for me than for you, because the Lord's hand has turned against me!"*

*14 At this they wept aloud again. Then Orpah kissed her mother-in-law goodbye, but Ruth clung to her. 15 "Look," said Naomi, "your sister-in-law is going back to her people and her gods. Go back with her." 16 But Ruth replied, "Don't urge me to leave you or to turn back from you. Where you go I will go, and where you stay I will stay. Your people will be my people and your God my God. 17 Where you die I will die, and there I will be buried. May the Lord deal with me, be it ever so severely, if even death separates you and me." 18 When Naomi realized*

> *that Ruth was determined to go with her, she stopped urging her. NIV*

This is wonderful because sometimes we believe that we do things that God would never want to use us in His Kingdom, but this is a story of the love of God for His people and the people that they love. The people of God recognized the dedication that Ruth had to Naomi and spoke to her about her seed.

> *Ruth 4:11-13 And all the people that [were] in the gate, and the elders, said, [We are] witnesses. The LORD make the woman that is come into thine house like Rachel and like Leah, which two did build the house of Israel: and do thou worthily in Ephratah, and be famous in Bethlehem: 12 And let thy house be like the house of Pharez, whom Tamar bare unto Judah, of the seed which the LORD shall give thee of this young woman. 13 So Boaz took Ruth, and she was his wife: and when he went in unto her, the LORD gave her conception, and she bare a son.*

After the son is born, the women begin to talk to Naomi about the blessing of that particular seed for this peculiar relationship of Ruth and Boaz.

> *Ruth 4:14-17 And the women said unto Naomi, Blessed [be] the LORD, which hath not left thee this day without a kinsman, that his name may be famous in Israel. 15 And he shall be unto thee a restorer of [thy] life, and a nourisher of thine old age: for thy daughter in law, which loveth thee, which is better to thee than seven sons, hath born him. 16 And Naomi took the*

*child, and laid it in her bosom, and became nurse unto it. 17 And the women her neighbours gave it a name, saying, There is a son born to Naomi; and they called his name Obed: he [is] the father of Jesse, the father of David.*

Now we get to list the holy seed up to King David. God has not said a word to anybody about David being their kind. If fact David has not been born yet, but the generation of the holy seed is mentions here in Ruth 4:18-22.

*Ruth 4:18-22 Now these [are] the generations of Pharez: Pharez begat Hezron, 19 And Hezron begat Ram, and Ram begat Amminadab, 20 And Amminadab begat Nahshon, and Nahshon begat Salmon, 21 And Salmon begat Boaz, and Boaz begat Obed, 22 And Obed begat Jesse, and Jesse begat David.*

And David is the seed that God would use to bring forth His seed through His son as recorded in Jeremiah 33:22.

*Jeremiah 33:22 As the host of heaven cannot be numbered, neither the sand of the sea measured: so will I multiply the seed of David my servant, and the Levites that minister unto me.*

And concerning Jesus Christ Paul mentions his status to the Romans as the seed of David in Rom 1:3.

*Romans 1:3 Concerning his Son Jesus Christ our Lord, which was made of the seed of David according to the flesh;*

This is one of the reasons that we should not judge people by what we see. Who would have thought God would elevate a person to the status of Ruth based on her background. If we are honest who would have thought that God would elevate us based on our background. I know that I am one of those persons that God did not look at where I came from or what I did in order to save me even from myself inflict- ed cuts and bruises based on disobedience, bad decisions and dishonorable deeds.

## People are Seed

We have already talked about when we mentioned the seed of Abraham. Isaac and Jacob are carriers of Abraham's seed in the natural and we enjoy the benefit of that same seed spiritually. However the example of Hanna, her husband Elkanah is an example of giving a person to God as a seed offering. We find that in 1Samuel 2:20.

> *1 Samuel 2:20 And Eli blessed Elkanah and his wife, and said, The LORD give thee seed of this woman for the loan which is lent to the LORD. And they went unto their own home.*

I cannot think of anyone else in the Bible that asked God for a person just to give back to Him. There may be someone but I have not run across that in my personal reading. This is a clear example of seedtime and harvest. They gave God Hanna's first born son as a seed and God gave her a harvest back in people because she and her husband sowed a per- son. The sowing of their son Samuel is recorded in 1Samuel 1:20.

> *1 Samuel 1: 20 Wherefore it came to pass, when the time was come about after Hannah had*

*conceived, that she bare a son, and called his name Samuel, saying, Because I have asked him of the LORD.*

And when Samuel was weaned, they give him to God as promised.

The next time that it was time to go to the Temple of God to give sacrifice and to worship God Hanna would not go until Samuel was weaned so that she could give her seed to God 1Samuel 1:22.

*1 Samuel 1:22 But Hannah went not up; for she said unto her husband, I will not go up until the child be weaned, and then I will bring him, that he may appear before the LORD, and there abide for ever.*

Wow, this is amazing to me to actually sow a person as seed. She was not expecting the harvest that she received, even though she knew what happens in the natural when you plant seed, she was not expecting a harvest of children. She was so happy that God had opened her womb that all she could do was to worship and praise God for His good- ness and mercy in giving her that one child. Hannah prayed and said in 1 Samuel 2:1,

*1 Samuel 2:1 And Hannah prayed, and said, My heart rejoiceth in the LORD, mine horn is exalted in the LORD: my mouth is enlarged over mine enemies; because I rejoice in thy salvation."*

She did not ask for any more children, however, she did not realize that the harvest of more children was coming. Look what happened in 1 Samuel 2:21.

***1 Samuel 2:21 And the LORD visited Hannah, so that she conceived, and bare three sons and two daughters. And the child Samuel grew before the LORD.***

Hannah had three sons and two daughters five for one. What if she had kept that one and changed her mind about sowing him unto God she may have had only that one.

Elkanah had children by his other wife but she did not choose to sow any of her children; however, he agreed with Hannah to allow her to sow hers. How do you come to a point where you are willing to give up your only son? Hannah was provoked by her enemy. Elkanah other wife knew that God has shut up Hannah's womb and tormented her because she had no children, but she overcame by the giving up of her only son to the LORD. That is what Mary did by willing going alone with the plan that God the Father has for her son Jesus who is God's seed to bring Him a harvest of all of the believers of Christ Jesus today and forever more.

**A Tenth As Spiritual and Natural Seed**

The spiritual connection giving a tenth, a tithe of all was first mentioned of Abraham giving that to Melchizedek, king of Salem. Abraham understood what needed to be done to uphold his part of the covenant meal. This is mentioned in Hebrews of the tithe that Abraham gave in Hebrews 7:2 and the covenant meal that Melchizedek brought to Abraham to share in Genesis 14:18.

*Hebrews 7:2 To whom also Abraham gave a tenth part of all; first being by interpretation King of righteousness, and after that also King of Salem, which is, King of peace;*

*Genesis 14:18 And Melchizedek king of Salem brought forth bread and wine: and he was the priest of the most high God.*

Now we see how Abraham was giving a seed to the Most High God. He gave a tenth of all. Abraham understood God's part of the covenant and his part of the covenant. God's part was to protect Abraham and his family in all of the places that traveled in his obedience in believing what God has said to him. Abraham was blessed in his health, his finances, protection from the kings and princes of the different lands etc.

At this time it was not called a tithe but a tenth. This is what helps us to understand what the tithe is, a tenth. Another person that wanted to get a covenant blessing from God was Jacob. When Jacob was leaving his family wondering when or if he would ever see them again made a promise to God to give God a tenth of all that God would give him in return for getting him back to his father's house in and when God did that then shall the LORD by his God.

*Genesis 28:21 - So that I come again to my father's house in peace; then shall the LORD be my God*

This is his request and he also gives God his commitment of a tenth of all that he is given by God as his part of the covenant.

*Genesis 28:22 And this stone, which I have set for a pillar, shall be God's house: and of all that thou shalt give me I will surely give the tenth unto thee.*

## The King's Seed

The natural connection was mentioned when Samuel was talking to God about the people wanting a king and God's reply to Samuel is found in this passage.

*1 Samuel 8:15-18 And he will take the tenth of your seed, and of your vineyards, and give to his officers, and to his servants. 16 And he will take your menservants, and your maidservants, and your goodliest young men, and your asses, and put them to his work. 17 He will take the tenth of your sheep: and ye shall be his servants. 18 And ye shall cry out in that day because of your king which ye shall have chosen you; and the LORD will not hear you in that day.*

This is not all that God told Samuel to warn the people of the thing that they would have to give up to a king, but this part is interesting because God is telling Samuel that the king that the people wanted was going to take a tenth of their seed and sheep. We know a tenth to be a tithe, there- fore the people were asking for God to be replaced as their King by a man that was going to take an additional tenth of their seed and sheep. They would still have to bring all of their offering to the temple according to the Law of Moses, but they wanted a covenant with a man to take over what God had been doing for them all of the time. Look at this now in 1 Samuel 8:19-20.

*1 Samuel 8:19-20 Nevertheless the people refused to obey the voice of Samuel; and they said, Nay; but we will have a king over us; 20 That we also may be like all the nations; and that our king may judge us, and go out before us, and fight our battles. KJV*

Part of their covenant with a king was to give him a tithe of all that they had and in return they would have someone to judge them and fight their battles. We are still talking about seed. They need seed to plant the crops for the next season and the next year but they were willing to give it up for something they already had working well for them. Samuel and God were trying to explain to the people their part of the covenant with a king. They refused to listen to the Lord and God said let them have a king.

It was not until years later and with the third king who was Solomon that the people came to understand what God was telling them. Solomon taxed the people greatly to support all of his issues, wives and concubines, but it was his son Rehoboam, when he became king that finally drove the people to the point where they could not take care of their own families. They asked King Rehoboam for relief but he refused and that split the kingdom and they were no longer one nation. Notice what happened as recorded in 1Kings 12:6-10.

*1 Kings 12:6-10 And king Rehoboam consulted with the old men, that stood before Solomon his father while he yet lived, and said, How do ye advise that I may answer this people? 7 And they spake unto him, saying, If thou wilt be a servant unto this people this day, and wilt serve them, and answer them, and speak good words to them, then they will be thy servants for ever. 8 But he forsook the counsel of the old men, which they had given him, and consulted with the young men that were grown up with him, and which stood before him: 9 And he said unto them, What counsel give ye that we may answer this people, who have spoken to me, saying, Make the yoke which thy father did put upon us lighter? 10 And the young men that were grown up with him spake unto him, saying, Thus shalt thou speak unto this people that spake unto thee, saying, Thy father made our yoke heavy, but make thou it lighter unto us; thus shalt thou say unto them, My little finger shall be thicker than my father's loins. KJV*

We can see from this event what happened in the natural but there is a spiritual side to this as well. Everything that God had said to them came to pass. They did not see it as a problem at first because they all were so prosperous and when the harvest came they did not recognize it.

# CHAPTER 4

# Christ "The Seed" In Jesus

Remember when God said to the serpent in Genesis 3:15.

***Genesis 3:15 And I will put enmity between thee and the woman, and between thy seed and her seed; it shall bruise thy head, and thou shalt bruise his heel.***

This was the beginning of our understanding that God was going to put things back in order and the holy seed would not be lost. God did not say when all this would happen however He knew the exact time. No one expected it would be as wonderful as it was going to be. When reading the Old Testament you can find instances where it talks about the coming Messiah and all of the things that He would do, but we have to understand what the most important thing that He did was to bring the holy seed back in right standing with God. It was the heart of God for His sons to be in good stand- ing with him and enjoy the relationship that Adam had before sin. So He watched over the holy seed until it could come into the earth and position those that would choose to be back in the Garden of Eden walking and talking with God.

Can you imagine God starting with the seed of Christ from the beginning so that we would have a perfect, holy and righteous seed?

*Galatians 3:16 Now to Abraham and his seed were the promises made. He saith not, And to seeds, as of many; but as of one, And to thy <u>seed</u>, which is <u>Christ</u>.*

Isaiah's portrayal of Christ is significant, but we still have to understand what we would be like as His seed. The prophecies of Christ are told in four categories. This is not all that was said but it will give us an understanding of what is in His seed because when we know what is in His seed, His bloodline we will understand what to expect to get from Him. The four categories of Christ are as follows:

**1. His History**

His history was first mentioned in Genesis chapter 3 as being the seed of the woman and later in Isaiah 7:14.

*Isaiah 7:14 Therefore the Lord himself shall give you a sign; Behold, a virgin shall conceive, and bear a son, and shall call his name Immanuel.*

This passage is giving us information about His miraculous conception and birth as the seed of Mary, his mother and He shall be called Immanuel which means god, god-like one, mighty one, mighty men, men of rank, mighty heroes, God, the one true God, Jehovah, mighty things in nature Strength (power) all of this is letting us know that it is God that is about to be born. God was sending His Word, which was His only begotten son.

*John 1:14 And the Word was made flesh, and dwelt among us, (and we beheld his glory, the glory as of the only begotten of the Father,) full of grace and truth.*

*Isaiah 7:15-16 Butter and honey shall he eat, that he may know to refuse the evil, and choose the good. 16 For before the child shall know to refuse the evil, and choose the good, the land that thou abhorrest shall be forsaken of both her kings.*

Abhorrest in the Hebrew means I.to be grieved, loathe, abhor, feel a loathing or abhorrence or sickening dread. He would be forsaken by the spiritual leaders and the natural leaders.

## 2. His Assignment – The Arm of the Lord Revealed

*Isaiah 53:2 For he shall grow up before him as a tender plant, and as a root out of a dry ground: he hath no form nor comeliness; and when we shall see him, there is no beauty that we should desire him.*

This is an indication that Christ will grow up tenderly, that He would be young, that he would be a root from a dessert place, a very dry place, he will have no form of His own, nor would he have any comeliness or beauty that those that see Him should desire. Now those of us who say we want to be like Christ this is what we should expect to be a part of His seed. When we position ourselves to live by faith, to love as God does, to be obedient to God's word people are not all going to like us, they are not going to like our ways nor is everybody going to celebrate us and be glad about the favor of God or the anointing of God that is on our lives because we choose to live for Him.

*Isaiah 53:3 He is despised and rejected of men; a man of sorrows, and acquainted with grief: and we hid as it were our faces from him; he was despised, and we esteemed him not.*

This also is what we can expect because it is in His seed. When we identify ourselves as followers of Jesus we should expect the same thing to happen to us because of Him, not because we are so wonderful, but because He was despised and rejected it is in our seed. Here is an example, there certain parts of the world where Christians are still persecuted, killed, destroyed, property seized and many have to go into hiding just to assemble together in church. That does not happen to any other religions; nobody bothers them because the seed that they follow is different.

Even in this country, you do not get into trouble when you mention any religious leader except Jesus. I remember as a child many years ago all of the religions at that time were mentioned in our history books, but not Christianity, it was not even mentioned as an afterthought. And what is so interesting that was a time when prayer was still allowed in school, we prayed, we read scripture but there was no mention of our God in our history text books, Jesus was completely rejected it was as if He was never existed in history.

Being rejected of men is in the seed of Christ so we must all get delivered from people, we are to love them but not make them our gods. So what if they do like us, we can't change people, so what if they think we are peculiar, we are, if they require us to choose activities that are against the word of God just to be friends with them we have to say no. There are many way that we can be rejected of men but cannot buy into things that would cause us also to reject our God, because if we are ashamed of the gospel that means that we want to be like the world so that we can be accepted. The world has rejected and is still rejecting the gospel of Jesus Christ.

> ***Isaiah 53:4 Surely he hath borne our griefs, and carried our sorrows: yet we did esteem him stricken, smitten of God, and afflicted.***

This is powerful principles that exist in the seed of God. Being affected of God is in the seed. It pleased the Father to afflict Him for us. It was extremely difficult for Him to be stricken and smitten as He had to do on the cross. He even asked His Father if there was any other way to do what He came to do and heaven was silent.

> ***Mark 14:36 And He said, "Abba, Father, all things are possible for You. Take this cup away from Me; nevertheless, not what I will, but what You will."***

Since that is in His seed we should expect as mature sons of God to suffer for the sake of others. Jesus was a living sacrifice. His physical body had to be sacrificed in order for us to have life. This is a part of what is in His seed.

Paul explained this to the Church of Rome in Romans 12:1.

> ***Romans 12:1 I beseech you therefore, brethren, by the mercies of God, that ye present your bodies a living sacrifice, holy, acceptable unto God, which is your reasonable service.***

Jesus' physical body (flesh) was sacrificed, however, we do not had to die to our flesh physically, we have to die spiritually to our flesh and let the things that are not of God go. It may sound simple but it is not. Sometimes people may hurt you so bad that you feel like you are dying and after that you have to forgive them and let that go. That is truly difficult without the help of the Holy Spirit. There are a lot of things that we may have to die to but for the sake of this part of the seed I will mention one significant one. Remember what Jesus said about how to treat your enemies in Matthew 5:43-45.

*Matthew 5:43-45 Ye have heard that it hath been said, Thou shalt love thy neighbour, and hate thine enemy. 44 But I say unto you, Love your enemies, bless them that curse you, do good to them that hate you, and pray for them which despitefully use you, and persecute you; 45 That ye may be the children of your Father which is in heaven: for he maketh his sun to rise on the evil and on the good, and sendeth rain on the just and on the unjust.*

Can you see how the seed has changed? The seed that we had inherited from Adam was unholy and we were allowed to hate our enemies, which was not of God. But now the seed of Christ is that we love our enemies and be like our God who allows the sun to shine of the evil and the good and the rain to rain on the evil and the good. Instead of beat- ing our enemies, hating them or doing evil to them, we have to love them just like we do our neighbor.

*Isaiah 53:5 But he was wounded for our transgressions, he was bruised for our iniquities: the chastisement of our peace was upon him; and with his stripes we are healed.*

This portion of the seed lets us know that we receive some things from Him that does not require us to do like the king, but is just for us to receive and be. It all comes with being the son of God. God used His own seed, his only begotten son to give us peace and healing is in this portion of His seed. A price had to be paid for us to have peace. He was wounded and bruised for our peace. In this passage, peace in the Hebrew is Shalom which means, completeness, soundness, welfare, peace, completeness (in number) safety, soundness (in body), welfare, health, prosperity, peace, quiet, tranquility, contentment, friendship of human relationships, with God especially in covenant relationship.

We are healed by the stripes and the blows that He took. Healing in this passage is rapha' which means to heal, make healthful, to heal, of God, healer, physician (of men), of hurts of nations involving restored favour (fig), of individual distresses (fig), Niphal) to be healed literal (of persons), of water, pottery, of national hurts (fig), of personal distress (fig), (Piel) to heal literal of national defects or hurts (fig), (Hithpael) in order to get healed. This is amazing to me because we are already healed, it is in the seed. We are not going to get healed we are healed because He paid the price for that.

After this Isaiah talks about the fact that we are like sheep have gone astray, we have turned away from God and the only way that we all can get the holy seed and its benefits is that God would use His only son to pay the price that we must pay to have peace and healing.

*Isaiah 53:6 All we like sheep have gone astray; we have turned every one to his own way; and the LORD hath laid on him the iniquity of us all.*

*Isaiah 53:7 He was oppressed, and he was afflict- ed, yet he opened not his mouth: he is brought as a lamb to the slaughter, and as a sheep before her shearers is dumb, so he openeth not his mouth.*

He knew the price He had to pay yet he did not open his mouth to mummer or complain about having to do this for someone else. It is in His seed to do for others and that is one of the expectations of those that follow Him.

*Isaiah 53:8 He was taken from prison and from judgment: and who shall declare his generation? for he was cut off out of the land of the living: for the transgression of my people was he stricken.*

God choose him for this assignment. It was not a happy or pleasant assignment but God needed it to be done by someone in the earth. I wonder how many of us know our assignment but do not want to go through the process to get the authority to do it because it is not pleasant or convenient.

*Isaiah 53:9 And he made his grave with the wicked, and with the rich in his death; because he had done no violence, neither was any deceit in his mouth.*

He was guilty of nothing that would cause him to have to die, yet we were guilty of everything possible and He choose to die for us to free us from the punishment (penalty), power and presence of our sin. We are free now in this dispensation and time period from the penalty and power of sin, but we will have to wait to be free of the presence of sin.

## 3. His Titles

He has so many titles that I cannot possibly name them all here, I can think of more 200 in the New Testament, how- ever I will mention a few just to help us identify some of the items that are in the seed.

> *Isaiah 9:6 For unto us a child is born, unto us a son is given: and the government shall be upon his shoulder: and his name shall be called Wonderful, Counsellor, The mighty God, The everlasting Father, The Prince of Peace.*

From this passage alone we can see that He is called:

- Wonderful
- Counsellor
- The Mighty God
- The Everlasting Father
- The Prince of Peace

> *Isaiah 8:8 And he shall pass through Judah; he shall overflow and go over, he shall reach even to the neck; and the stretching out of his wings shall fill the breadth of thy land, O Immanuel.*

In this passage, He is called:

- Immanuel

   *Revelation 1:8 I am Alpha and Omega, the beginning and the ending, saith the Lord, which is, and which was, and which is to come, the Almighty. In this passage He declares of Himself I am:*

- Alpha and Omega

- The Beginning and the Ending

- The Almighty

   *Matthew 1:1 The book of the generation of Jesus Christ, the son of David, the son of Abraham. And in this passage He is called:*

- The Son of David

- The son of Abraham

   *Mark 10:33 ..... the Son of man shall be delivered unto the chief priests, and unto the scribes; ..... In this passage He is called:*

- The Son of Man

   *1 Timothy 6:14-15 That thou keep this commandment without spot, unrebukeable, until the appearing of our Lord Jesus Christ: 15 Which in his times he shall shew, who is the blessed and only Potentate, the King of kings, and Lord of lords;*

- King of kings o Lord of lords

## 4. His Characteristics

His Characteristics are as numerous as His titles but I will share a few for the sake of us recognizing some of the things that are in His seed.

*Isaiah 42:2 He shall not cry, nor lift up, nor cause his voice to be heard in the street.*

He is:

- Quiet

*Isaiah 42:3 A bruised reed shall he not break, and the smoking flax shall he not quench: he shall bring forth judgment unto truth.*

He is:

- Gentle
- Brings judgment unto Truth

*Isaiah 42:4 He shall not fail nor be discouraged, till he have set judgment in the earth: and the isles shall wait for his law.*

He:

- Cannot Fail
- Cannot Be Discouraged
- Perseveres

*Isaiah 42:5 Thus saith God the LORD, he that created the heavens, and stretched them out; he that spread forth the earth, and that which cometh out of it; he that giveth breath unto the people upon it, and spirit to them that walk therein:*

He gives:

- Breath

- Spirit

*Isaiah 42:6 I the LORD have called thee in righteousness, and will hold thine hand, and will keep thee, and give thee for a covenant of the people, for a light of the Gentiles;*

He is:

- A Covenant Giver

- Light Giver

*Isaiah 42:7 To open the blind eyes, to bring out the prisoners from the prison, and them that sit in darkness out of the prison house.*

He:

- Opens Blind Eyes to bring out of prison

- Brings from Darkness

*1 Peter 2:25 For ye were as sheep going astray; but are now returned unto the Shepherd and Bishop of your souls.*

He is:

- The Bishop of our Souls
- The Shepherd

> *John 6:33 For the bread of God is he which cometh down from heaven, and giveth life unto the world.*

He is:

- True Bread From Heaven
- Giver of life unto the World

> *John 6:35 And Jesus said unto them, I am the bread of life: he that cometh to me shall never hunger; and he that believeth on me shall never thirst.*

He is:

- Bread of Life

# Chapter 5

# The Seed of Abraham

He is the seed of Abraham and we have already covered Abraham's seed but this part is noteworthy so we will cover it here and that is our flesh. As Christians were are always talking about battling our flesh and that is because we do not want it cut off. But it must be cut off if we are going to grow in the things of God and come into the maturity that God desires for all of us.

God addressed this flesh covenant with Abraham. The Bible does not say why He needed this done when He introduce this to him as a part of the covenant with his people. But it He did say those that did not have the flesh cut off would themselves be cut off from His people.

> *Gen 17:9-11 And God said unto Abraham, Thou shalt keep my covenant therefore, thou, and thy seed after thee in their generations. 10 This is my covenant, which ye shall keep, between me and you and thy seed after thee; Every man child among you shall be circumcised. 11 And ye shall circumcise the flesh of your foreskin; and it shall be a token of the covenant betwixt me and you. From this we understand that the flesh has to go. It has to be removed and once that happens it is separated from the person and it dies. It cannot live separated from the person.*

> *All of this is in the seed of Abraham and is pass on to us through Jesus Christ.*

In addition, God allowed the child to wait eight days before it had to be done. So, when we are saved God understands that we will need time to get rid of our flesh. He also understands that we will need a spiritual Father like Abraham to cut it off of us until we are mature enough in Christ to recognize it and cut it off ourselves, or go and get it cut. We know that this covenant between Abraham and God to circumcise the males is a natural physical act. But the God wants us to get rid of our spiritual flesh which comes from the unholy seed and replace it with His holy seed. The Bible goes on to say in Genesis 17:12-14.

> *Genesis 17-12-14 And he that is eight days old shall be circumcised among you, every man child in your generations, he that is born in the house, or bought with money of any stranger, which is not of thy seed. Gen 17:13 He that is born in thy house, and he that is bought with thy money, must needs be circumcised: and my covenant shall be in your flesh for an everlasting covenant. Genesis 17:14 And the uncircumcised man child whose flesh of his foreskin is not circumcised, that soul shall be cut off from his people; he hath broken my covenant.*

That anyone that will not cut off their flesh has broken the covenant. Now I can imagine the women saying that is not for me. Yes, it is because there is no gender in Christ, there is no male or female. We are all sons of God and we are all the bride of Christ male and female, therefore we must come to understand that we must cut or kill our in the flesh.

Abraham was ninety years old when God introduced this to him and he was willing to let it go. We have to be like that today and be willing let it go. Notice in Genesis 17:24.

*Genesis 17:24 And Abraham was ninety years old and nine, when he was circumcised in the flesh of his foreskin that Abraham did not even question God He just did it.*

The New Testament is prolific with discussion of the flesh and getting rid of it. One example can be found in Philippians 3:3.

*Philippians 3:3 For we are the circumcision, which worship God in the spirit, and rejoice in Christ Jesus, and have no confidence in the flesh.*

And another in 1 Peter 3:18.

*1 Peter 3:28 For Christ also hath once suffered for sins, the just for the unjust, that he might bring us to God, being put to death in the flesh, but quickened by the Spirit:*

This is the understanding that we have; Christ Jesus gave up his body of flesh that we might have eternal life. He had to get rid of the corruptible body and receive an incorruptible body. This lets us know that we have to do this in the spirit and in the natural. Even if we do not die a physical death before Jesus returns we will still have to give up this flesh body for an eternal incorruptible body. We see that in the following passage.

> *1 Corinthians 15:42 So also is the resurrection of the dead. It is sown in corruption; it is raised in incorruption:*

We have to give up the flesh body we received from Adam because the seed sown of this body was of dishonor and we see that in 1 Corinthians 15:43.

> *1 Corinthians 15:43 It is sown in dishonour; it is raised in glory: it is sown in weakness; it is raised in power:*

So that our body can be raised in glory, it says here that it was sown in weakness and it will be raised in power. Our natural body has to be given up for a spiritual body and we have to be aware that both exist a natural and a spiritual body we see that in 1 Corinthians 15:44.

> *1 Corinthians 15:44 It is sown a natural body; it is raised a spiritual body. There is a natural body, and there is a spiritual body.*

We know that it is written in Genesis that the first Adam became a living soul Genesis 2:7.

> *Genesis 2: 7 And the LORD God formed man of the dust of the ground, and breathed into his nostrils the breath of life; and man became a living soul.*

But we are saved by the seed of the second Adam who was made a quickening spirit, not became but was made.

> *1 Corinthians 15:45. And so it is written, The first man Adam was made a living soul; the last Adam was made a quickening spirit.*

Paul talks to us about the fact the first body of Adam must be natural of the earth and the second spiritual the Lord from heaven in 1 Corinthians 15:46-48.

*1 Corinthians 15:46-48 Howbeit that was not first which is spiritual, but that which is natural; and afterward that which is spiritual. 47 The first man is of the earth, earthy: the second man is the Lord from heaven. 48 As is the earthy, such are they also that are earthy: and as is the heavenly, such are they also that are heavenly.*

Even though we are born in the image of the earth, we shall bear the image of heaven. Flesh and blood cannot inherit the kingdom of God, nor can corruption inherit incorruption. We are the sons of God and we must inherit from His seed and not from an unholy seed. We have to get rid of flesh and blood and be made flesh and bone incorruptible.

*1 Corinthians 15:49-50 And as we have borne the image of the earthy, we shall also bear the image of the heavenly. 50 Now this I say, brethren, that flesh and blood cannot inherit the kingdom of God; neither doth corruption inherit incorruption.*

We shall all be changed that belong to God because we must in order to inherit from Him and our understanding of this begins with understanding the cutting of the unneeded flesh of Abraham. Jesus Christ is called the seed of Abraham. He died to the flesh, the unneeded part, just as Abraham had cut his unneeded flesh off so that he and the people of God could be changed. We shall be changed because the corruptible flesh has died. This is a mystery but what a blessing to be able to understand the mystery. Paul explains it to the church of Corinth in the following passages.

> *1 Corinthians 15:51-55 Behold, I shew you a mystery; We shall not all sleep, but we shall all be changed, 52 In a moment, in the twinkling of an eye, at the last trump: for the trumpet shall sound, and the dead shall be raised incorruptible, and we shall be changed. 53 For this corruptible must put on incorruption, and this mortal must put on immortality. 54 So when this corruptible shall have put on incorruption, and this mortal shall have put on immortality, then shall be brought to pass the saying that is written, Death is swallowed up in victory. 55 O death, where is thy sting? O grave, where is thy victory?*

Abraham was also a lord. The seed of lord, not God but a lord (man) in the earth, he owned so much property, not land but animals, tents and people (servants) and all the things they needed that he must have looked like a small city traveling around. The word lord in the Hebrew is 'adown which means firm, strong, lord, master, and in reference to men in means superintendent of household, affairs, master, king. In English, the word lord means some- one or something having power, authority, or influence; a master or ruler. Other names for lord that are synonyms: magnate, tycoon, captain, baron or king just to name a few.

I said all that to say the lord is in the seed of Abraham and Jesus Christ is his seed and He is now Lord of lords. Just in case you are wondering where it says that Abraham is called a lord in the Bible let's take a look at a few passages. The first is the one we are all familiar with,

## THE IMPORTANCE OF SEED

when his wife Sarah called him lord. Well most will say she was his wife so that does not count. Yes, it does because she used the same word lord and this indicates that he was lord over more than his wife. This is mentioned in Genesis 18:12.

*Genesis 18:12 Therefore Sarah laughed within herself, saying, After I am waxed old shall I have pleasure, my lord being old also?*

After death other people called him lord. This is mentioned when he was looking to purchase a place to bury her. He requested this from them and they answered thus:

*Genesis 23:5-6 And the children of Heth answered Abraham, saying unto him, 6 Hear us, my lord: thou art a mighty prince among us: in the choice of our sepulchres bury thy dead; none of us shall withhold from thee his sepulchre, but that thou mayest bury thy dead."*

They all called him lord because they said hear us my lord and they said that he was a mighty price among them and that is what a lord is when it pertains to men or women. During this same discussion and conversation, a Hittite that lived there with the children of Heth did own a field with a cave on it offered to give Abraham the cave to bury her and in the process of doing this he called Abraham lord. We see that in Genesis 23:10-11.

*Genesis 23:10-11 And Ephron dwelt among the children of Heth: and Ephron the Hittite answered Abraham in the audience of the children of Heth, even of all that went in at the gate of his city, say- ing, 11 Nay, my lord, hear*

> *me: the field give I thee, and the cave that is therein, I give it thee; in the presence of the sons of my people give I it thee: bury thy dead.*

But Abraham would not take it for free. This is my thinking, the Bible does not say but I believe that Abraham did not want anybody to take credit for what God had given; he was willing to pay for everything. This is the only place in the Bible where Abraham actually purchases property. He was traveling through the land that God had promised to his seed believing God but not actually taken physical posses- sion of it. It already belonged to him because God had given him and his seed the land for an everlasting possession. Abraham's purchase of the field with the cave on it to bury his wife is recorded in Genesis 23:12-13.

> *Genesis 23:12-13 And Abraham bowed down him- self before the people of the land. 13 And he spake unto Ephron in the audience of the people of the land, saying, But if thou wilt give it, I pray thee, hear me: I will give thee money for the field; take it of me, and I will bury my dead there.*

Abraham was willing to sacrifice his only begotten son that God recognized as his holy seed. Isaac, Abraham's only begotten son, was willing to be the sacrifice. The seed of this deed was in the seed of Abraham and Jesus is called the seed of Abraham; therefore, this seed was available to him. Abraham's actions in this event had to happen in the earth before Jesus Christ could actually do it. It had to already be in the bloodline of the holy seed. Abraham planted the seed and the record of this seed planting is found in Genesis 22:2.

*Genesis 22:2 And he said, Take now thy son, thine only son Isaac, whom thou lovest, and get thee into the land of Moriah; and offer him there for a burnt offering upon one of the mountains which I will tell thee of.*

Now God was asking Abraham to take the only son, holy seed, and sacrifice it to Him as a burnt offering. That meant that Abraham and his son had to be willing to do that. Abraham left immediately to obey God in this matter. He knew that God had told him that Isaac was going to be the seed that would enable him to be the father of many nations, so he must have thought that God was going to raise him from the dead because he told the servants that were with them that he and the boy would be back after the sacrifice.

*Genesis 22:4-5 Then on the third day Abraham lifted up his eyes, and saw the place afar off. 5 And Abraham said unto his young men, Abide ye here with the ass; and I and the lad will go yonder and worship, and come again to you.*

Abraham considered that act of obedience an act of worship and prepared to sacrifice Isaac.

*Genesis 22:6 And Abraham took the wood of the burnt offering, and laid it upon Isaac his son; and he took the fire in his hand, and a knife; and they went both of them together.*

Notice that gave the task of carrying the wood not really knowing what God had said to his father asked his father about the sacrifice.

*Genesis 22:7 And Isaac spake unto Abraham his father, and said, My father: and he said, Here am I, my son. And he said, Behold the fire and the wood: but where is the lamb for a burnt offering?*

Abraham's reply did not answer the question in Genesis 22:8.

*Genesis 22:8 And Abraham said, My son, God will provide himself a lamb for a burnt offering: so they went both of them together.*

And they continued to the place of sacrifice and Abraham prepared to sacrifice Isaac his only son the seed that the nations from Abraham would emerge.

When Isaac found out that he was the sacrifice he agreed. Isaac was not a babe or a small child because he was able to carry that heavy load of wood, now the son is the sacrifice for all of the nations that would come from Abraham.

*Genesis 22:9-10 And they came to the place which God had told him of; and Abraham built an altar there, and laid the wood in order, and bound Isaac his son, and laid him on the altar upon the wood. 10 And Abraham stretched forth his hand, and took the knife to slay his son.*

This is powerful because that is exactly what Jesus would have to do for His father Jehovah. Once God saw that Abraham and Isaac were both willing to obey him God spoke to Abraham.

## THE IMPORTANCE OF SEED

> *Genesis 22:11-12 And the angel of the LORD called unto him out of heaven, and said, Abraham, Abraham: and he said, Here am I. 12 And he said, Lay not thine hand upon the lad, neither do thou any thing unto him: for now I know that thou fearest God, seeing thou hast not withheld thy son, thine only son from me.*

Now we have an example in the earth that demonstrated what God the Father and Christ his son would do for us by both being willing to do their part. The father willing to sacrifice his son and his son willing to be the sacrifice was a part of the seed that was in Abraham. He was the Father of many nations and he would not be able to number the people that would come from his seed as he would not be able to count the sand of the sea shore or the stars in the night sky. He truly represented the Father's position. Isaac, on the other hand, had to be the obedient son willing to be the sacrifice at the instruction of his father.

Once Abraham raised his arm to slay his son as the sacrifice God spoke to him again and called him twice and instruct- ed him not to lay hands on the boy, then God showed him the sacrifice that He had provided.

> *Genesis 22:13-14 And Abraham lifted up his eyes, and looked, and behold behind him a ram caught in a thicket by his horns: and Abraham went and took the ram, and offered him up for a burnt offer- ing in the stead of his son. 14 And Abraham called the name of that place Jehovah Jireh: as it is said to this day, In the mount of the LORD it shall be seen.*

This seed has now been established in Abraham and Isaac. This is an act that they had to do together. Now that this seed has been established God spoke again to Abraham about his obedience.

*Genesis 22:15-16 And the angel of the LORD called unto Abraham out of heaven the second time, 16 And said, By myself have I sworn, saith the LORD, for because thou hast done this thing, and hast not withheld thy son, thine only son: 17 That in blessing I will bless thee, and in multiply- ing I will multiply thy seed as the stars of the heaven, and as the sand which is upon the sea shore; and thy seed shall possess the gate of his enemies.*

This is profound because this is what Jesus will do for us the number of people that cannot be counted that follow him. He gave up his life as a sacrifice with the help and instructions from his father. Then God begin to talk to Abraham again about his seed and Jesus Christ is called the Seed of Abraham.

*Genesis 22:18 And in thy seed shall all the nations of the earth be blessed; because thou hast obeyed my voice.*

This is what Jesus would do, he would obey his Father and the whole world was going to be saved. Jesus mentioned this obedience to His Father and he mentioned His commitment to His father in John 5:19.

*John 5:19 Then answered Jesus and said unto them, Verily, verily, I say unto you, The Son can do nothing of himself, but what he seeth the*

## THE IMPORTANCE OF SEED

*Father do: for what things soever he doeth, these also doeth the Son likewise.*

Isaac was prepared to obey his father and did and must have had to submit his will to his father's will to obey God. Jesus said in John 5:30.

*John 5:30 I can of mine own self do nothing: as I hear, I judge: and my judgment is just; because I seek not mine own will, but the will of the Father which hath sent me.*

God sent Abraham to the mountain to sacrifice his son and that is exactly what Abraham set out to do his assignment from God to sacrifice his seed, Isaac with full agreement of his son (seed) and their obedience caused them to plant the scarifying of only son seed that we enjoy today because of the sacrifice of Jesus Christ. Jesus is called the Seed of Abraham.

## Chapter 6

## The Seed of David (The King)

Remember what God told Samuel to tell the people about what to expect from a king and still they rejected God as their king and wanted a king on earth to be like the other people who had kings but did not have God. Everything that God warned them about happened to them via the kings, yet God used this opportunity to establish kingship through David so that He could get back into His position as King to His people just as He used Abraham to establish Himself as Lord to His people.

As we begin this discussion about the seed of King David let's take a look at what God said about kings long before Samuel or David.

This is so interesting to me because God knew that the people would ask for a king and gave specific directions concerning the king and the kingdom. Moses was the one that gave the people the first information about their kings. This is utterly amazing to me because God told them when their earthly king would come on the scene and how he should handle himself.

In Deuteronomy Chapter 17, God has Moses explain to the people that when they came in possession of the land that God had promised them, they were going to ask for a king and when they did God gave these directions to the people:

- The Lord thy God shall Choose
- Must be one of thy brethren
- Must not be a stranger that is not thy brethren

God gave these directions to the coming kings:

- He shall not multiply horses to himself
- Not cause the people to return to Egypt so that he can multiply horses
- Neither shall he multiply wives to himself
- Neither shall he greatly multiply to himself silver and gold
- When he sitteth upon the throne of his kingdom, that he shall write him a copy of this law in a book out of that which is before the priests the Levites
- he shall read therein all the days of his life: that he may learn to fear the LORD his God, to keep all the words of this law and these statutes, to do them
- That his heart be not lifted up above his brethren, and that he turn not aside from the commandment, to the right hand, or to the left
- to the end that he may prolong his days in his kingdom, he, and his children, in the midst of Israel

This is amazing to me because they did not have to guess what kind of king God wanted to rule and reign over His people. It is very clear in this passage what God wanted here in Deuteronomy 17:14-20.

*Deuteronomy 17:14-20 When thou art come unto the land which the LORD thy God giveth thee, and shalt possess it, and shalt dwell therein, and shalt say, I will set a king over me, like as all the nations that are about me; 15 Thou shalt in any wise set him king over thee, whom the LORD thy God shall choose: one from among thy brethren shalt thou set king over thee: thou mayest not set a stranger over thee, which is not thy brother. 16 But he shall not multiply horses to himself, nor cause the people to return to Egypt, to the end that he should multiply horses: forasmuch as the LORD hath said unto you, Ye shall henceforth return no more that way 17 Neither shall he multiply wives to himself, that his heart turn not away: neither shall he greatly multiply to himself silver and gold. 18 And it shall be, when he sitteth upon the throne of his kingdom, that he shall write him a copy of this law in a book out of that which is before the priests the Levites: 19 And it shall be with him, and he shall read therein all the days of his life: that he may learn to fear the LORD his God, to keep all the words of this law and these statutes, to do them: 20 That his heart be not lifted up above his brethren, and that he turn not aside from the commandment, to the right hand, or to the left: to the end that he may prolong his days in his kingdom, he, and his children, in the midst of Israel. KJV*

When you look at what God wants in a king for the people and how He wants the king to be one of their brethren, we understand how to evaluate what happened to the kingdom of Israel. There were plenty of examples of kings from the Gentile nations that did not have the call or the character that God wanted for His people but it seems that their example had more weight and influence than the commandments of God.

God did not want the king to multiple horses unto himself not send the people back to Egypt (into bondage) so that he could multiply horses to himself. God told the people never to go back to Egypt. God also said for the kings not to multiply to him silver and gold and not to multiply wives to him. God said for the king to write a copy of His commandments of the book that was before the Priest and the Levites and keep them ever before him. In addition, he was to also do the commands that were written in the copy that was written and not to life himself above his brethren. None of the Gentile kings had this set of rules to follow.

In fact, most of them did whatever they knew to do. They gathered great wealth in horses, silver and gold; they had as many wives as they wanted, some even had harems (the part of the house separate private quarters reserved for wives and concubines). Many gathered together great armies and almost all evaluated themselves above their brethren.

David, however, was different because he loved God, His commandments and His people. He was a shepherd and he knew how to take care of the people of God, he did not gather great wealth for himself at the expense of the people of God. So much so that God chose him to establish a kingly throne in the earth forever. To that end God sent the Prophet Nathan to give David this information. We find all of this in 2 Samuel 7:16-19.

*2 Samuel 7:16-19 And thine house and thy kingdom shall be established for ever before thee: thy throne shall be established for ever. 17 According to all these words, and according to all this vision, so did Nathan speak unto David. 18 Then went king David in, and sat before the LORD, and he said, Who am I, O Lord GOD? and what is my house, that thou hast brought me hitherto? 19 And this was yet a small thing in thy sight, O Lord GOD; but thou hast spoken also of thy servant's house for a great while to come. And is this the manner of man, O Lord GOD*

David's Character:

- Integrity as a Shepherd - God choose David to take care of His people because of the integrity of his heart and the skillfulness of his hand.

    *Psalm 78:70-72 He chose David also his servant, and took him from the sheepfolds: 71 From following the ewes great with young he brought him to feed Jacob his people, and Israel his inheritance. 72 So he fed them according to the integrity of his heart; and guided them by the skillfulness of his hands. KJV*

According to this scripture David was a man of integrity. According to the dictionary definition integrity is the quality of being honest and having strong moral principles; moral uprightness. The Hebrew word for integrity here in this passage is tom which means completeness, fullness, innocence and simplicity. All of this is in the seed of David.

Integrity as a King David fought off all of the enemies of the people until he brought the nation of Israel to a place of Peace. We can see in 2 Samuel 3:18.

> *2 Samuel 3:18 Now then do it: for the LORD hath spoken of David, saying, By the hand of my servant David I will save my people Israel out of the hand of the Philistines, and out of the hand of all their enemies. KJV*

Saving the people of God from all of their enemies is in the seed of David.

Integrity as a Servant of God – God mentions this in the word that He sent to Jeroboam in 1 Kings 14:8.

> *1 Kings 14:8 And rent the kingdom away from the house of David, and gave it thee: and yet thou hast not been as my servant David, who kept my commandments, and who followed me with all his heart, to do that only which was right in mine eyes; KJV*

God is saying here that David kept His commandments and followed Him with all of His heart. This is also in the seed of David and is what God required of a king that would rule over His people.

Integrity with the wealth he received 2 Samuel 8:10-11.

> *2 Samuel 8:10-11 Then Toi sent Joram his son unto king David, to salute him, and to bless him, because he had fought against Hadadezer, and smitten him: for Hadadezer had wars with Toi. And Joram brought with him vessels of silver, and ves- sels of gold, and vessels of brass: 11*

> *Which also king David did dedicate unto the LORD, with the silver and gold that he had dedicated of all nations which he subdued; KJV*

David dedicated the silver and gold that he received from the nations that he subdued to the LORD. Now God knows that He can trust him with the wealth that was put into his hands. This is also a part of the seed in the seed of David.

David himself talked about his obedience to what God had told him in regards to the desire of his heart to build a house for the Ark of the Covenant. David had dedicated the money, silver and gold to the LORD. God did not say any- thing to him about it in the beginning when he first started to set the funds aside but much later God let him know that he could not do that because he was a man of war.

> *1 Chronicles 28:2 Then David the king stood up upon his feet, and said, Hear me, my brethren, and my people: As for me, I had in mine heart to build an house of rest for the ark of the covenant of the LORD, and for the footstool of our God, and had made ready for the building: 3 But God said unto me, Thou shalt not build an house for my name, because thou hast been a man of war, and hast shed blood. He was a man of war. KJV*

David obeyed and did not complain. His obedience is in his seed.

Many of the attributes that God has said that He wanted a king to have that ruled over His people are found in the life and character of David. He kept the commandments of God. He did not multiply himself with horses, silver or gold. He did not put extra burdens on the people so that he could increase his own wealth, thus keeping them from going back into bondage, specifically Egypt.

David's throne was mentioned by God by name in Isaiah 9:7.

> *Isaiah 9:7 Of the increase of his government and peace there shall be no end, upon the throne of David, and upon his kingdom, to order it, and to establish it with judgment and with justice from henceforth even for ever. The zeal of the LORD of hosts will perform this.*

And his lineage was also mentioned by name in Isaiah 11:1.

> *Isaiah 11:1 And there shall come forth a rod out of the stem of Jesse, and Branch shall grow out of his roots: Jesse was the father of David and He would be a King forever from the seed of King David.*

## Chapter 7

## Jesus The Son of Man – (Natural and Spiritual) Seed

Everything that we need is in His (Jesus Christ) seed. Seed is extremely important. God used it from the beginning to help us in every way possible. We cannot avoid the process of the principle of seed even if we tried. You may think that you deserve everything or nothing but what seed did you plant. That will determine what you get. It is a fail proof system. You can plant anything in the natural or in the spirit and you are going to get that back nobody, can stop it, nobody can change, nobody can rearrange it even Satan himself. God has put a system in place to prosper us and protect us that cannot be altered. All we have to do is plant the seed we want and wait for the harvest.

Jesus Christ is the ultimate SEED; this is what He was trying to give us understanding of from the beginning. In the naturel the earth does not produce seed; its purpose is to assist in growing the seed. As it is in the natural so is it in the spirit because the natural has to come first Paul talks about that in 1 Corinthians 15:46.

> *1 Corinthians 15:46 Howbeit that was not first which is spiritual, but that which is natural; and afterward that which is spiritual.*

And because of this I believe that everything that God has created in the natural has a spiritual message and the message of the seed in that of Jesus Christ Isaiah mentions this about Jesus in Isaiah 53:10.

*Isaiah 53:10 Yet it pleased the LORD to bruise him; he hath put him to grief: when thou shalt make his soul an offering for sin, he shall see his seed, he shall prolong his days, and the pleasure of the LORD shall prosper in his hand.*

If you go to Isaiah 53 and read verses 1-9, you will see all the mean, harsh and evil things that happened to Jesus and you will also see that He did not say a word, He did not open His mouth to complain, rebuke, or mummer because He knew He was the seed that was going to change the world. He knew that the harvest would not be something that the Devil could stop and He purposed to plant that holy seed so that the harvest could come.

In spite of all that He had to go through it pleased the LORD to bruise him. This is something we have to understand, it was the LORD that put him to grief so that He could make his soul an offering for sin. After this, Isaiah mentioned that He shall see His seed and He shall prolong his days. This act of seedtime and harvest put those that want it in position be a part of the family of God and to come into His presence sin free. You cannot come into the presence without of the penalty of sin be paid for and at the end of verse 10 Isaiah says that the pleasure of the LORD shall prosper in his hand.

Since we understand that seed reproduces after its own kind, we were not able to plant a sinless seed. In order to get a sin free harvest, God knew this from the beginning and He began to talk to us about it when he mentioned to the Serpent representing the Devil in the Garden of Eden in Genesis 3:15 about the seed of the woman crushing his head. It was the seed of Jesus Christ that was going to crush him. Isaiah goes on to say in Isaiah 53:11.

> ***Isaiah 53:11 He shall see of the travail of his soul, and shall be satisfied: by his knowledge shall my righteous servant justify many; for he shall bear their iniquities.***

To us that this is the seed is the righteous servant that will justify many. This holy seed will bear our iniquities. This is a tremendous blessing because the Hebrew word for "their iniquities" is avon meaning our perversity (willful, stubbornness, obstinacy), our depravity (corruption, wickedness, immorally), our great guilt, our punishment of iniquity the consequence of iniquity. This is the seed (iniquity) that were planting and we need to plant a holy seed to get rid of all of these weeds that are coming up as a result of sin. He would have to be one of us in order to plant the seed for us. God knew that therefore He mentions in Isaiah 53:12.

> ***Isaiah 53:12 Therefore will I divide him a portion with the great, and he shall divide the spoil with the strong; because he hath poured out his soul unto death: and he was numbered with the transgressors; and he bare the sin of many, and made intercession for the transgressors.***

This means that He would take the punishment, received the consequences and make intercession for us. He did all of that on his way to the cross and at the cross.

What a wonderful Savior we have in Jesus Christ, He saved our seed with His seed and now we can come boldly before the throne of Grace.

What is in the holy seed? The entire natural and the spiritual seed of whatever was in the line of people that were in the process of His coming were passed down from generation to generation. The gospel of Matthew presents Jesus Christ as King. If we look at that in Matthew, we can see in the genealogy of Jesus Christ and take note of what is in the seed of the King in Matthew 1:1.

***Matthew 1:1 The book of the generation, of Jesus Christ, the son of David, the son of Abraham.***

The Hebrew word for generation is in the verse is genesis which means beginning. Notice in verse 1 He begins with being the son of David the king first, and then the son of Abraham the father and lord and a man of faith. It is very clear that God wants us to focus to king David and Father Abraham. We have mentioned the characteristics of both men and their relationship with God. It is also clear that everything that is in their seed is passed down generation after generation naturally and spiritually.

When we study the lives of David and Abraham we often refer to the parts where they missed the mark associated with their sin issues. David has some very interesting drama in his life. One of which was stealing a man's wife and having him killed so he could marry her and one item in Abraham's life was the kings of the land that his wife was his sister to protect himself. All of this was in the seed and it was passed down. Have you ever wondered why God did not seem to be so concerned about these kinds of things that he would remove their assignment from them? Well it was because God was not worried about sin and He knew the seed of Jesus Christ would settle the sin issue once and for all and completely remove that from His blood line so that none that took on His blood would have that issue.

When we think of the people of God especially those that attend a church we think that they should all be wonderful. There should not be anybody doing anything outside of the word of God. And many people get hurt in church because their expectation is that everyone has had their mind renewed to the mind of Christ and all of those iniquity seeds in their natural blood line are gone. The truth is that there is no sin in the bloodline of Jesus Christ, however, when we become saved and take on His bloodline, we have to work out our soul salvation, we have to go through the process to become sons of God in our deeds. Being born in the family of God does not automatically mean that we have His character in the natural. We have to be transformed into His character and God give us the power to do that in John 1:12-13.

*__John 1:12-13 But as many as received him, to them gave he power to become the sons of God, even to them that believe on his name: 13 Which were born, not of blood, nor of the will of the flesh, nor of the will of man, but of God.__*

Notice the emphases of being born of God not of man. This allows those that received Him to work on the issues that they have to overcome. This is exciting because it frees them from the punishment of sin and from the power of sin. Jesus Christ took care of all of those issues.

As we continue to look at the genealogy of Jesus Christ, we begin to find some interesting people many of which would not be selected by the church of today because our expectation of people is greater than they are able to perform or even bear. While Jesus freed us from the penalty and consequences of having to pay the spiritual price of our sin, thus allowing us to spend eternity with God and not have to go to hell.

As we talked about before God knew that we could not pay that price so He took care of that for us, however there are things that we may do in the natural the effect of which is definitely going to cause a consequence. For example, if people participate in an activity that will cause pregnancy not really planning the pregnancy to occur, the result of that may cause the pregnancy to happen even if it was not intended, even if the persons repent and admit that they should not have done that.

One more example, if someone gets angry with another person for what they consider a serious reason and during that time of anger breaks out the windows the other persons car, the windows are broken and there is no way to change that so even if the persons finds out that they made a mistake about what was done to cause the problem, ever if they regret what they did, even if the car attacks was the wrong car. We can ask the person and God for forgiveness and receive that forgiveness, even though being forgiven positions you as if you never commit- ted the act, the physical damage has still been done and you have to replace all of the car windows.

I said all of that to say this, God knew that He would have to reconcile us from every sin possible, so the sin problem was not an issued when it came to selecting the people that would be in the genealogy of Jesus Christ. When we take a look at the genealogy of Jesus Christ, you will be amazed at the people in the lineup that would not have been selected by people today to be there. See Matthew 1:2-16.

> **Matthew 1:2-3 Abraham begat Isaac; and Isaac begat Jacob; and Jacob begat Judah and his brethren; 3 And Judah begat Phares and Zara of Thamar; begat Aram; and Phares begat Esrom; and Esrom begat Aram;**

Judas is one that would not be chosen because of his help- ing his brothers plan to kill another one of his brothers and eventually sold him into slavery, this is in the seed of the bloodline. Thamar is one that would not have been selected because of her posing as a prostitute in order to have an intimate relationship with her father-in-law. This is in the seed of the bloodline.

> **Matthew 1:4-6 4 And Aram begat Aminadab; and Aminadab begat Naasson; and Naasson begat Salmon; 5 And Salmon begat Booz of Rachab; and Booz begat Obed of Ruth and Obed begat Jesse; 6 And Jesse begat David the king; and David the king begat Solomon of her that had been the wife of Urias;**

Ruth would not have been chosen because she came from the family of Lot and was the result of his biological daughter incest with him, this is in the seed of the bloodline. This lady's children would not have been chosen because of her affair with King David. We know what her name was but in this passage God called her the wife of Urias, the husband that was deliberately put in the front line of a war so that he would be killed. This is in the seed of the bloodline.

*Matthew 1:7-16 7 And Solomon begat Roboam; and Roboam begat Abia; and Abia begat Asa; 8 And Asa begat Josaphat; and Josaphat begat Joram; and Joram begat Ozias; 9 And Ozias begat Joatham; and Joatham begat Achaz; and Achaz begat Ezekias; 10 And Ezekias begat Manasses; and Manasses begat Amon; and Amon begat Josias; 11 And Josias begat Jechonias and his brethren, about the time they were carried away to Babylon: 12 And after they were brought to Babylon, Jechonias begat Salathiel; and Salathiel begat Zorobabel; 13 And Zorobabel begat Abiud; and Abiud begat Eliakim; and Eliakim begat Azor; 14 And Azor begat Sadoc; and Sadoc begat Achim; and Achim begat Eliud; 15 And Eliud begat Eleazar; and Eleazar begat Matthan; and Matthan begat Jacob; 16 And Jacob begat Joseph the husband of Mary, of whom was born Jesus, who is called Christ.*

I have name only a few but there are more in this genealogy that can be mentioned. All that was in them was in the seed of Jesus; however, none of it was in the seed of Christ. Jesus had to concur and overcome all of the generational curses passed down until the time of His birth. You have to break a generational curse before a child is born in order for that child not of have that in their seed. This is such a bless- ing for us because once we accept Jesus as Lord and Savior all of the curses attached to His bloodline from previous generations were broken. His seed is pure and holy and it is His bloodline that covers and protects us. In addition, because He broke all those generational cures and purified the seed we know how to break the seed of generational curses.

Jesus was the first one to do that. Now we know how to do that because of His example.

I have some things that have been passed down through my generation that I definitely want to get rid of. One of which, that is broken and that is to have children out of wedlock and single mothers raising children alone. There are others but that one was so obvious. You may have some as well. These are curses that have been passed down the person. That is challenged with it may not have been the one to start it. I have talked to people who are challenged with that that have visible manifestation such as alcohol and gossip as well as invisible things like pornography or jealously. People who want to get rid of some challenges in their lives really struggle if they are not aware of generational curses. You cannot just quit those; you have to break it from your entire bloodline. It is wonderful to know that you can get rid of those kind of things that is present in the seed that is passed down for generation.

By now you may be asking where in the Bible is there an example of bad seed being passed down through Jesus' bloodline that was not corrected. Let us take a look at a few. Remember when Abraham, when his name was still Abram told his wife to lie about being his wife to save him from harm in Genesis 12:10-13.

> ***Genesis 12:10-13 And there was a famine in the land: and Abram went down into Egypt to sojourn there; for the famine was grievous in the land. 11 And it came to pass, when he was come near to enter into Egypt, that he said unto Sarai his wife, Behold now, I know that thou art a fair woman to look upon: 12 Therefore it shall come to pass, when the Egyptians shall see thee,***

*that they shall say, This is his wife: and they will kill me, but they will save thee alive. 13 Say, I pray thee, thou art my sister: that it may be well with me for thy sake; and my soul shall live because of thee.*

Now after his name was changed to Abraham, he did the same thing again in Genesis 20:2.

*Genesis 20:2 And Abraham said of Sarah his wife, She is my sister: and Abimelech king of Gerar sent, and took Sarah.*

Abraham passed this bad seed down through his bloodline to his son Isaac who did the exact same thing. We can see that in Genesis 26:6-7.

*Genesis 26:6-7 And Isaac dwelt in Gerar: 7 And the men of the place asked him of his wife; and he said, She is my sister: for he feared to say, She is my wife; lest, said he, the men of the place should kill me for Rebekah; because she was fair to look upon.*

Let's look at one more example of Abraham and Sarah. Remember earlier God said the king should have only one wife. Abraham is not a king but he is a lord. Abraham and Sarah decided to add another wife to Abraham. This means that he married Hagar also and now he has two wives. They passed that down through their bloodline. It skipped Isaac but did not skip Isaac's two sons Esau and Jacob. They both had more than one wife. Jacob had two wives and this seed kept going down through the generations until it reached King David. And by now it has multiplied.

David begins to marry for a lot of different reasons other than just wanting a wife. He married for political reasons and this seed was passed down to his son Solomon. David married Michal, Ahinaoam, Abigail, Maacah, Haggith, Abital, Eglah, and Bathsheba, the wife of Uriah. The account of most of these wives can be found in 2 Samuel chapters 3 and 5. Solomon married so many that I cannot name them all, since he had 700 wives and 300 concubines. This is mentioned in 1 Kings 11:3-4.

***1 Kings 11:3-4 And he had seven hundred wives, princesses, and three hundred concubines: and his wives turned away his heart. 4 For it came to pass, when Solomon was old, that his wives turned away his heart after other gods: and his heart was not perfect with the LORD his God, as was the heart of David his father.***

Can you see the danger and the tragedy of bad seed? I do not think that any one of these persons set out to do this on purpose. It happened because of the seed planted by prior generations. I do not want you to completely misunderstand the point; we are talking about passing down generational bad seed. However, it is possible for you and me to start a generational curse by committing a sin and refusing to repent from that particular thing.

God knew this about us and sent the pure and holy seed of His only begotten son to help us overcome this problem. There are many good natural things that we pass down generation to generation but we have to realize that things are first real in the spirit rather than in the natural. You say why is that? It is because God is a spirit and He created everything and since He created everything it was done in the spirit before it was done in the natural. And since we have to live here on earth in the natural I believe that is why God made sure that everything here in the earth represents some spiritual truth. I know you are now asking is there scripture to back that up your belief. Yes, there is and it is in John 1:12.

***John 1:12 But as many as received him, to them gave he power to become the sons of God, even to them that believe on his name:***

We that receive Jesus Christ are born into the family, and of course at that point, we do not really care how God's system works. We are just glad to be one in the number. But according to John 1:12, we are given the power to become sons that look and act like God, not just be born of God but to be like Him in thought, word and deed.

The word power in the Greek is **exousia <u>which means power of choice, liberty of doing as one pleases, leave or permission, physical and mental power, the ability or strength with which one is endued, which he either possesses or exercises, the power of authority (influence) and of right (privilege), the power of rule or government (the power of him whose will and commands must be submit- ted to by others and obeyed) universally authority over mankind, specifically the power of judicial decisions, of authority to manage domestic affairs, metonymically, a thing subject to authority or rule, jurisdiction one who possesses authority, a ruler, a human magistrate, the lead- ing and more powerful among created beings superior to man, spiritual potentates, a sign of the husband's authority over his wife, the veil with which propriety required a women to cover herself, the sign of regal authority, a crown.</u>**

All of this is spiritual authority, not natural strength; this is what the Apostle John wrote about in John 1:1-3.

***John 1:1-3 In the beginning was the Word, and the Word was with God, and the Word was God. 2 The same was in the beginning with God. 3 All things were made by him; and without him was not any thing made that was made.***

This is talking about a fact that nothing was made without the word of God which is Christ, and more important Jesus Christ to us all that receive Him or call on His name. All of this is in the spirit before it was in the natural. God Himself is so great and powerful we cannot even imagine how great He is. But look at what he gave us to become his son. All of that authority and power as defined by the word exousia is not intended for us to use just in the natural. It is spiritual authority that has the ability to tell natural things what to do.

We do receive some things are we consider as good in our seed. For example, some of us think that long eyelashes are beautiful, if that is passed down through the seed of the generations before us we may think that is good. But that is not what God made sure that we all had. The good seed is what we all need. Sometimes we think that we are good because we don't curse or drink or gossip or treat people badly etc. But Jesus said that none are good except God, and that is because of what is in our seed. So how can we get only the good seed? We get that by the blood of the Lamb of God Jesus Christ.

What was it in Abraham's seed that God wanted to be passed down? Let's take a look. Abraham was a man of faith and God wanted that to be passed down (Jesus Christ is the author and the finisher of our faith).

Abraham was a good father and also the father of a number that cannot be counted. God, our Father in heaven, is the Father of all of us, Father of a number that cannot be counted. God wanted that to be passed down (God is a good Father). Abraham was the head of his family, he did not look for another man in the earth to take care of his responsibility. God wanted that to be passed down (Jesus Christ is the head of God's family and took total responsibility to do what needed to be done in the earth to make that happen).

Abraham trusted God and left to go where God wanted him to go even though did not tell him where he was going. God only gave him the direction. God wanted that passed down (Jesus completely trusted God His Father). Abraham protected what God put in his hands, including fighting five kings to get his nephew Lot back from their capture. God wanted that passed down (God has given His people authority to take dominion over the kingdoms of this world and we can do that because of Jesus Christ. (Because "The kingdoms of this world are become the kingdoms of our Lord, and of his Christ; and he shall reign for ever and ever.)

Abraham gave a tithe of all and God wanted that passed down. Abraham made a covenant with God and he kept his part believing God to keep his part and God wanted that passed down (we have a blood covenant with God that can- not be broken). Abraham believed that God had given him all that God had promised him even though he did not physically see ninety percent of what God said that He had given him. He never saw the millions of people that would come from his seed but he believed God for them and God want- ed that passed down (we enjoy the blessing of Abraham even though he never knew any of us personally). He offered his only son as a sacrifice to God and then believed God to raise him from the dead and God wanted that passed down (Jesus Christ was God only begotten son that He sacrificed for our sin and God raised Him from the dead).

He pleaded for the salvation of Sodom and Gomorrah and God was willing to save them if He could find ten righteous. God could not find ten, but He wanted that compassion that Abraham had for those that were lost to be passed down (God save the whole world for one righteous in the person of Jesus Christ). Abraham participated in the bread and wine covenant meal, which we now call communion with Melchizedek and God wanted that passed down (Christians are to participate in the communion as often as we remember the body and blood of Jesus Christ).

There is much more but I think that you get the point. So when you want to be too hard on yourself remember, God knows what He has put in the seed of Jesus and He also knows what is in your seed. He still wants you and I and God loves us beyond our ability to understand it. God wants us to be a part of His family and enjoy the benefits of being His sons. God had this in mind before the foundations of the world and there is nothing that we could ever "do or not do" that would cause God to change His mind or break the covenant that He made with Abraham and David on our behalf.

What was in David's seed that God wanted passed down? Let's name a few! David worshiped God in instrumental music and song and God wanted that passed down.

> ***Psalm 150:5 Praise him upon the loud cymbals: praise him upon the high sounding cymbals.***

## THE IMPORTANCE OF SEED

*Psalm 102:18 This shall be written for the generation to come: and the people which shall be created shall praise the LORD.*

David was a man of war that was willing to fight to protect those who would or could not protect themselves and God wanted that passed down.

*1 Samuel 17:50 So David prevailed over the Philistine with a sling and with a stone, and smote the Philistine, and slew him; but there was no sword in the hand of David.*

David was a shepherd and was willing to take care of sheep that could not take care of themselves even to the point of his own hurt and God wanted that passed down.

*2 Samuel 24:17 And David spake unto the LORD when he saw the angel that smote the people, and said, Lo, I have sinned, and I have done wickedly: but these sheep, what have they done? let thine hand, I pray thee, be against me, and against my father's house.*

David honored God order and was not willing to harm God delegated authority, King Saul, God's anointed even though that person was trying to kill him and God wanted that passed down.

*1 Samuel 24:6 And he said unto his men, The LORD forbid that I should do this thing unto my master, the LORD'S anointed, to stretch forth mine hand against him, seeing he is the anointed of the LORD.*

David trusted God to help him win battles when the odds seem to be against him and God wanted that passed down.

> *1 Samuel 23:2 Therefore David enquired of the LORD, saying, Shall I go and smite these Philistines? And the LORD said unto David, Go, and smite the Philistines, and save Keilah.*

> *2 Samuel 2:1 And it came to pass after this, that David enquired of the LORD, saying, Shall I go up into any of the cities of Judah? And the LORD said unto him, Go up. And David said, Whither shall I go up? And he said, Unto Hebron.*

David honored his word to his closest friend Jonathan and God wanted that passed down.

> *2 Samuel 9:1 And David said, Is there yet any that is left of the house of Saul, that I may shew him kindness for Jonathan's sake?*

David had a tinder heart for God's people and was willing and able to teach them the ways of the LORD and God wanted that passed down.

> *Ezekiel 37:24 And David my servant shall be king over them; and they all shall have one shepherd: they shall also walk in my judgments, and observe my statutes, and do them.*

David gathered men that nobody would have given a chance and changed their lives, men that had been determined to be outcast and shaped them into a mighty army and God wanted that passed down.

*1 Samuel 22:2 And every one that was in distress, and every one that was in debt, and every one that was discontented, gathered themselves unto him; and he became a captain over them: and there were with him about four hundred men.*

David ruled the kingdom that God put his hands to with integrity and God wanted that passed down.

*1 Kings 9:4 And if thou wilt walk before me, as David thy father walked, in integrity of heart, and in uprightness, to do according to all that I have commanded thee, and wilt keep my statutes and my judgments:*

David spent intimate time with God and God wanted that passed down. All you have to do is read the Psalms to see the many intimate moments that he had with the LORD and one of those moments was in Psalm 63:1.

*Psalm 63:1 O God, thou art my God; early will I seek thee: my soul thirsteth for thee, my flesh longeth for thee in a dry and thirsty land, where no water is;*

David trusted God to be his shepherd and God wanted that passed down.

*Psalm 23:1 The LORD is my shepherd; I shall not want.*

David was willing to serve the King and God wanted that passed down.

*1 Samuel 16:21 And David came to Saul, and stood before him: and he loved him greatly; and he became his armourbearer.*

David purposed in his heart to put a great deal of the wealth that God had given him into the building of a temple for God. He also encouraged the leaders of Israel to do the same and God wanted that passed down. Notice the vast- ness of the money and precious metals and precious stones that David accumulated in 1 Chronicles 29:1-11.

*1 Chronicles 29:1-5 Furthermore David the king said unto all the congregation, Solomon my son, whom alone God hath chosen, is yet young and tender, and the work is great: for the palace is not for man, but for the LORD God. 2 Now I have pre- pared with all my might for the house of my God the gold for things to be made of gold, and the silver for things of silver, and the brass for things of brass, the iron for things of iron, and wood for things of wood; onyx stones, and stones to be set, glistering stones, and of divers colours, and all manner of precious stones, and marble stones in abundance. 3 Moreover, because I have set my affection to the house of my God, I have of mine own proper good, of gold and silver, which I have given to the house of my God, over and above all that I have prepared for the holy house, 4 Even three thousand talents of gold, of the gold of Ophir, and seven thousand talents of refined silver, to overlay the walls of the houses withal: 5 The gold for things of gold, and the silver for things of silver, and for all manner of work to be made by the hands of artificers. And who then is willing to consecrate his service this day unto the LORD?*

*1 Chronicles 29:6-11 Then the chief of the fathers and princes of the tribes of Israel, and the captains of thousands and of hundreds, with the rulers of the king's work, offered willingly, 7 And gave for the service of the house of God of gold five thou- sand talents and ten thousand drams, and of silver ten thousand talents, and of brass eighteen thou- sand talents, and one hundred thousand talents of iron. 8 And they with whom precious stones were found gave them to the treasure of the house of the LORD, by the hand of Jehiel the Gershonite. 9 Then the people rejoiced, for that they offered willingly, because with perfect heart they offered willingly to the LORD: and David the king also rejoiced with great joy. 10 Therefore David blessed the LORD before all the congregation: and David said, Blessed be thou, LORD God of Israel our father, for ever and ever. 11 Thine, O LORD, is the greatness, and the power, and the glory, and the victory, and the majesty: for all that is in the heaven and in the earth is thine; thine is the kingdom, O LORD, and thou art exalted as head above all.*

This is a long passage to read but it illustrates the love that David had for God and the House of God. Putting God first was something that David did regularly. Whenever God needed to correct him, once he knew that what he did was against God, he never did that again. It is no wonder that Jesus is mentioned so many times in the New Testament as the Son of David.

## Chapter 8

## The Seed of Jesus Christ

The people of God are the seed of Jesus Christ. It is easy to see and understand that seed is very important. It is mentioned 279 in the King James Version of the Bible. It clearly qualifies as a most mentioned item. From the first mention of seed in Genesis 1:11.

> ***Genesis 1:11 And God said, Let the earth bring forth grass, the herb yielding seed, and the fruit tree yielding fruit after his kind, whose seed is in itself, upon the earth: and it was so."***

This verse helps us understand how seed works. The last mention of seed in Revelation 12:17.

> ***Revelation 12:17 And the dragon was wroth with the woman, and went to make war with the remnant of her seed, which keep the commandments of God, and have the testimony of Jesus Christ."***

God had the people of God in mind.

The seed in the Old Testament Covenant leads us to the seed of the New Testament Covenant. It is so important that we understand who we are as the seed of Jesus Christ and when we do our lives will change significantly. We will no longer be a bad steward of words; we would be completely confident of what we have coming to us based on the word of God and even our own words, we will no longer blame other people for things that happen good or bad especially if we can remember the seed that we plant.

We can really see the importance of this when examine that in Revelation 12:17. It is the last scripture that mentions seed in the King James Version of the New Testament. Let us take a look and some of the key words in this verse:

- The first key word is "Dragon" the Greek word for Dragon is "Drakōn" which means dragon, a great serpent, a name for Satan. This is interesting because the serpent, representing Satan is the one that God spoke to in Genesis 3:15. Remember what God said to the serpent?

*Genesis 3:15 And I will put enmity between thee and the woman, and between thy seed and her seed; it shall bruise thy head, and thou shalt bruise his heel.*

Satan did not know who the seed was when God spoke this to him in Genesis 3:15, now that he does know he is angry (wroth) with the woman.

- The second key word is "Woman." The Greek word for woman in this verse is "Gynē" which means a woman of any age, whether a virgin, or married, or a widow a wife of a betrothed woman. The Hebrew meaning of woman in Genesis 3:15 is the same the Greek meaning in this verse. Who is this woman? Why is Satan angry with her? It is because she is the bride of Christ and she is producing the seed of Jesus Christ.

- The third key word is "War". The Greek word for war is "polemos", which means war, a fight, a battle, a dispute, strife, and quarrel. This verse says that Satan went to make war with the remnant of her seed. Why did Satan go to make war with the remnant of her seed? And why only a remnant of her seed? It is because he wants to stop the commandments of God.

- The fourth key word is "Remnant". The Greek word for remnant is "loipos" which means remaining, the rest, the rest of any number or class under consideration with a certain distinction and contrast, the rest, who are not of a specific class or number the rest of the things that remain. Now we know that these are the ones that are left. What happened to the rest?

- The fifth key word is "Seed". The Greek word for seed is "sperma" which means "from which a plant germinates the seed" i.e. the grain or kernel which contains within itself the germ of the future plants of the grains or kernels sown metaph, a seed i.e., a residue, or a few survivors reserved as the germ of the next generation, (just as seed is kept from the harvest for the sowing), the semen virile the product of this semen, seed, children, offspring, progeny family, tribe, posterity whatever possesses vital force or life giving power of divine energy of the Holy Spirit operating within the soul by which we are regenerated. This definition is similar to the Hebrew definition except it includes the Holy Spirit. Notice it is called the small portion (remnant), a few survivors reserved for the next generation.

- The six key word is "Commandments". The Greek word for commandments is "entolē" which means an order, command, charge, precept, injunction that which is prescribed to one by reason of his office, a commandment, a prescribed rule in accordance with which a thing is done, a precept relating to lineage, of the Mosaic precept concerning the priesthood ethically used of the commandments in the Mosaic law or Jewish tradition. This is talking about the commandments of God. It is very interesting that the remnant that of the woman's seed that the Satan went to make war with are those few that keep the commandment. Why these? It is because keeping the commandments of God will be a part of their seed. The commandments of God are the words of God and God's word will always produce what it says. Satan does not want the word of God to be a vital part of the life that we live because that will be passed down in our seed and he knows that those that keep the commandments love God not him and they will not be defeated by him when they live by and stand on the word. Satan is after the word of God because the word of God is seed. Loving God means that you have committed your life to Him. Jesus mentions that these are the ones that love Him in John 14:15. There are benefits for those who love God and one of those benefits is found in John 14:21-23.

*John 14:21-23 He that hath my commandments, and keepeth them, he it is that loveth me: and he that loveth me shall be loved of my Father, and I will love him, and will manifest myself to him. 22 Judas saith unto him, not Iscariot, Lord, how is it that thou wilt manifest thyself unto us, and not unto the world John 14:23 Jesus answered and said unto him, If a man love me, he will keep my words: and my Father will love him, and we will come unto him, and make our abode with him.*

Believers understand that God loves us. We understand that from John 3:16, that the Holy Spirit is in us and that we are the temple of God, but we have to love God if we want Him to love us and abide with us. When Jesus said my Father will love him, the love in the Greek is agapaō which means when speaking of persons to welcome, to entertain, to be fond of, and to love dearly or when speaking of things to be well pleased, to be contented at or with a thing.

We do not have to do anything for God to love us but to love to abide with us is a great benefit. I dearly love the presence of God. I talk to Him all day long and sometimes in my sleep, but He is not always happy to talk to me because of some of the things that I do or some of the things that I fellowship with and I can tell when God is not pleased. God is not shy; He will tell you when you do something not of Him, especially if you know the word of God and you choose not to obey. That makes me sad and as a result I do try to start the process of getting rid of (die to) the things that would cause me not to keep His commandments and love Him as I should. It is easy to love God because He loved me first but it is more difficult to love Him just because of who He is and keep His commandments as a commitment of my love for him, under all conditions and circumstances, no matter what I think, no matter who like it or not. That requires a trust in God that is also difficult if you are a person who trust has been broken by every authority figure in your life or if trust was just not an important issue in family dynamics etc. I want God to be pleased with me and I want Him working with me in everything that I do, how about you.

- The seventh key word is "God". The Greek word for God is "theos" which means the Godhead, trinity God the Father, the first person in the trinity Christ, the second person of the trinity Holy Spirit, the third person in the trinity, spoken of the only and true God refers to the things of God his counsels, interests, things due to him whatever can in any respect be likened unto God, or resemble him in any way God's representative or vice regent of magistrates and judges.

- This is the Godhead and we know that the fullness of the Godhead is in us, but sometimes it seems that God is nowhere near us because of the things that we encounter. It is hard for us to even imagine, not to mention believe that we are victorious. It is the tradition of men, the religious ideas and the things of this world that cause us not to want to obey the commandments of God. Jesus gives us some understanding of that is in Colossians 2:8-11.

*Colossians 2:8-11 Beware lest any man spoil you through philosophy and vain deceit, after the tradition of men, after the rudiments of the world, and not after Christ. 9 For in him dwelleth all the fulness of the Godhead bodily. 10 And ye are complete in him, which is the head of all principality and power: 11 In whom also ye are circumcised with the circumcision made without hands, in putting off the body of the sins of the flesh by the circumcision of Christ:*

We have the fullness of the Godhead through Christ in us and we are complete in Him. Yet we do not see ourselves according to this word over our lives. We are still trying to please the people that we have decided to love more than we love God. Christ is the head of principality and power and we have no need to fear anything or anybody, so what if they do not celebrate you, God will, so what if they do not love you, God does and he will always provide someone to love you no matter what you think about yourself.

- The eighth key word is "testimony". The Greek word for testimony is "martyria" which means a testifying, the office committed to the prophets of testifying concerning future events, what one testifies, testimony, i.e. before a judge. Remember, we are still talking about the dragon was wroth with the woman, and went to make war with the remnant of her seed, which keep the commandments of God, and have the testimony of Jesus Christ. Satan is out to terrify those that hear God and do not think that they do, that is his supposed opportunity to silence them. Many times they need conformation from someone of something else before they settle and believe that it was God. Those who keep His commandments will also have a testimony of Him. They will get information that someone needs and some- times what they need personally.

- When you spend intimate time with God you are able to get through some things that you thought would never happen and when you do you have a testimony of Jesus Christ because you kept God's commandments and you love Him you will find yourself being circumcised (circumcise is in the seed from Abraham) of all off the unneeded flesh that you can let go. Remember, you have to be ready to let the flesh go and being in the presence of God abiding with Him positions you to get ready to let it go and then God cuts it and you move on to the next thing. You cannot testify of something that you have no evidence

## THE IMPORTANCE OF SEED

of, therefore it is not practical for you or me to tell someone how to get out of or through something that we have never been through, but it is very beneficial to be able to show someone what to do and how to get through.

- Have you ever had an occasion to ask someone for directions when you were driving in unfamiliar territory? If the person you asked has been down that road before they can not only give you street names but also landmarks. They almost want to give you too much information but people who have never been there before may sometimes give directions that have missing pieces and you have to guess your way to your destination. We need clear directions and understanding from God and it is important that we have a testimony that can be used by others. Who must the testimony be of? It must be of Jesus Christ.

- The ninth key word is "Jesus". The Greek word for Jesus "Jeusus", "Iēsous", Jesus = "Jehovah is salvation", Jesus, the Son of God, the Saviour of mankind, God incarnate. Sometimes we do not want to obey God because we say that Jesus is God so it is much easier for God to obey God than for us to do it. But God was made flesh so that we could see that this can be done by us. The example of Jesus bring- ing His flesh under control if clear for us to see.

*John 1:14 And the Word was made flesh, and dwelt among us, (and we beheld his glory, the glory as of the only begotten of the Father,) full of grace and truth.*

Remember the Word of God is also seed and it was made flesh, he went through everything that we go through and it is His testimony that lets us know that we can do what He did and it is our testimony that will let other people know that they can do what we did. When we give our testimony we know without a doubt that it was all God. And once we become transparent and tell it at God direction, they will also know that it was undeniable God that help you through. I have many testimonies like that but I will share one with you.

My youngest son was attacked with diabetes when he was 18 months old. His blood sugar was at 800 or 900 when we got to the hospital. The hospital staff was watching me because they thought that he was going to die in my presence. I never considered that he would die even thought I was backslidden at the time. When he did not die, they were so amazed they sent for other doctors to come and see the miracle. I am sure that they wanted to give themselves credit but I know that was undeniably God. As they proceeded with their treatment, they did not want to bring the blood sugar down too fast and they told me that they had no med- ical examples to go by and that he was so young and not much body weight (as an 18 month old would be). Then they sent for some student doctors to come and see and I was busy getting aggravated instead of thanking God for his life. I did not want my child to be a spectacle to medical community. Then something else happened. They were sup- posed to be giving him 3 units of insulin on a systematic time schedule. But they had never had to treat anyone like that before. They did not have syringes with easy markings, so one of the nurses gave him 30 units instead of 3 and he immediately fell unconscious. She ran to get help and she thought he was going to die. But he is still here and he is 35 years old now and doing well.

When that happened and God kept him alive, I had no problem thanking God for his life. The nurse thought that I was going to sue the hospital because of what she had done. But I told her my son is alive what am I going to sue you for he has his life. I cannot ask for more than that. I know and understand that this was all God. He should have been dead according to the information that they (hospital and doctor) had. Many people have died as adults with blood sugar 500 or less. This is my testimony of Jesus Christ. What is your testimony?

- This is the tenth key word "Christ". The Greek word for Christ is "Christos", Christ = "anointed" Christ was the Messiah, the Son of God anointed. This is the source of the seed.

We are still talking about the last mention of the word seed in the Book of Revelation. God gave John this information and in the beginning He gave us some specific information that will help us know how important the Seed is to His seed. See Revelation 1:1-3.

*Revelation 1:1-3 The Revelation of Jesus Christ, which God gave unto him, to shew unto his servants things which must shortly come to pass; and he sent and signified it by his angel unto his servant John: 2 Who bare record of the word of God, and of the testimony of Jesus Christ, and of all things that he saw. 3 Blessed is he that readeth, and they that hear the words of this prophecy, and keep those things which are written therein: for the time is at hand.*

We realize that there are many things that is revealed to John in the Book of Revelation which is the revelation of Jesus Christ. But the subject and topic of our study in this book is seed. John is talking about being the person that bare record of the word of God (seed) and the testimony of Jesus Christ of all of the things that he saw and he goes on to say that we are blessed if we read, hear and keep the words of this prophecy. This certainly applies to all that is recorded in the book of Revelation, but in particular also in Revelation 12:17.

***Revelation 12:17 And the dragon was wroth with the woman, and went to make war with the remnant of her seed, which keep the commandments of God, and have the testimony of Jesus Christ."***

Now we can see why Satan is angry with God's woman, the church, which is also the bride of Christ. And he makes war with her seed that keep the commandments of God and have the testimony of Jesus Christ.

## Chapter 9

# The Seed of the New Testament

Seed is mentioned in the New Testament so many different times but it is always trying to portray some spiritual truth. As we go through this topic, it is going to be very apparent of the importance of seed as an illustration of a particular spiritual truth. There is a wealth of information in the New Testament that will help us prosper. The seeds that we plant create our tomorrow. They are the harvest of our next season.

The next questions are how can we created our harvest and who is in charge our seed? The seed has in it what it needs to grow and prosper. So what happens to cause us not to get a good crop? Remember, Satan is after the seed so we must be aware of that and protect our seed from misuse and abuse by planting it in good ground. We are the ground that receives our seed (the Word of God). We have to prepare our mind to receive and understand the word of God and protect it from information that will cause our ground to be bad for growing seed.

Let us take a look at some examples of receiving our seed in Bad Ground:

> *Matthew 13:19 When any one heareth the word of the kingdom, and understandeth it not, then cometh the wicked one, and catcheth away that which was sown in his heart. This is he which received seed by the way side.*

You can get in lots of trouble if you are too young in Christ to understand the word of the kingdom you are hearing. One of the reasons that we do not understand the word of the kingdom is because we are still in the church. When John the Baptist, the forerunner of Jesus, mentioned what was coming he called the people to repent, turn from the old and turn to the kingdom in Matthew 3:1-2.

> *Matthew 3:1-2 In those days came John the Baptist, preaching in the wilderness of Judaea, 2 And saying, Repent ye: for the kingdom of heaven is at hand.*

Jesus taught the same thing. There are many instances in the book of Matthew where Jesus talks about the kingdom and how to operate in it. He is the King of kings. And He gave us, his subjects, some directions that we do not even acknowledge. One rule of the kingdom Jesus taught is in Matthew 6:33.

> *Matthew 6:33 But seek ye first the kingdom of God, and his righteousness; and all these things shall be added unto you.*

This is great, but I remember coming up in church from my childhood to my adulthood being taught the latter part of this scripture but not this part. Matthew 6:33 says seek first the kingdom of God and then all these things will be added. What things? They are found in Matthew 6:28- 32.

> *Matthew 6:28-32 And why take ye thought for raiment? Consider the lilies of the field, how they grow; they toil not, neither do they spin: 29 And yet I say unto you, That even Solomon in all*

> *his glory was not arrayed like one of these. 30 Wherefore, if God so clothe the grass of the field, which to day is, and to morrow is cast into the oven, shall he not much more clothe you, O ye of little faith? 31 Therefore take no thought, saying, What shall we eat? or, What shall we drink? or, Wherewithal shall we be clothed? 32 (For after all these things do the Gentiles seek:) for your heavenly Father knoweth that ye have need of all these things.*

I cannot say for you but I was taught that all I have to do was have faith. None of the churches that I attended mentioned to me about knowing the kingdom rules and obeying, I saw it there but I ignored it because everybody else did. Yet, when I heard the words of the kingdom there was no understanding of them on my part that gave the enemy ample opportunity to snatch away that word that sown in my heart. You can find out about the rules of the kingdom, the attitudes of the kingdom, what the kingdom is like, how to fellowship with fellow believers in the kingdom, how to do business in the kingdom and more in the book of Matthew because the book of Matthew is all about Jesus being King and His Kingdom.

The kingdom of God is a mystery to unbelievers and those who are not interested in knowing. When Jesus' disciples, the twelve and some of the multitude that he had just taught to ask what the parable meant he said to them in Matthew 13:11.

> *Matthew 13:11 He answered and said unto them, Because it is given unto you to know the mysteries of the kingdom of heaven, but to them it is not given.*

Even as a believer you have to be hungry enough to want to know the answers to particular mysteries. One example of what the kingdom is like is mentioned by Jesus in Matthew 13:44.

> **Matthew 13:44 Again, the kingdom of heaven is like unto treasure hid in a field; the which when a man hath found, he hideth, and for joy thereof goeth and selleth all that he hath, and buyeth that field.**

Once this man understood the revelation of the kingdom, he sold out to God, he sold everything and bought into the kingdom of heaven, he knew that there was nothing greater than this. It is time for us to learn about the kingdom, to live by the kingdom rules, and to obey the King Jesus Christ. Once we do that, we will never again receive our seed by the way side and allow anyone to misuse or abuse of our seed.

We all understand that we are the body of Christ, thus the church of the living God. Now we can't get stuck on the word church. Jesus called us the church but we are citizens of His kingdom, not the church. The word church literately is just a group of people gathered together for a common purpose. There are no rules or regulations or commandments regarding the church, all of those are in the Kingdom. Church is mentioned by name even by Jesus, but only to describe the group. One of the times that Jesus mentions church was when he was talking to Peter in Matthew 16:18.

> **Matthew 16:18 And I say also unto thee, That thou art Peter, and upon this rock I will build my church; and the gates of hell shall not prevail against it.**

The Greek word for church in this verse is ekklēsia which means a gathering of citizens called out from their homes into some public place, an assembly, an assembly of the people convened at the public place of the council for the purpose of deliberating, the assembly of the Israelites, any gathering or throng of men assembled by chance, tumultuously, in a Christian sense an assembly of Christians gathered for worship in a religious meeting, a company of Christian, or of those who, hoping for eternal salvation through Jesus Christ, observe their own religious rites, hold their own religious meetings, and manage their own affairs, according to regulations prescribed for the body for order's sake those who anywhere, in a city, village, constitute such a company and are united into one body, the whole body of Christians scattered throughout the earth, the assembly of faithful Christians already dead and received into heaven.

The book of Hebrews also shed some light on this in Hebrews 1:8.

*Hebrews 1:8 But unto the Son he saith, Thy throne, O God, is for ever and ever: a sceptre of righteousness is the sceptre of thy kingdom.*

And even in the prayer that we call the Lord's Prayer we say thy kingdom come on earth as it is in heaven not let thy church come on earth as it is in heaven. We see that in Matthew 6:9-10.

*Matthew 6:9-10 After this manner therefore pray ye: Our Father which art in heaven, Hallowed be thy name. 10 Thy kingdom come. Thy will be done in earth, as it is in heaven.*

**Matthew 13:20-21 But he that received the seed into stony places, the same is he that heareth the word, and anon with joy receiveth it; 21 Yet hath he not root in himself, but dureth for a while: for when tribulation or persecution ariseth because of the word, by and by he is offended.**

You can kill your seed by not wanting to deal with the pain that comes because of the word that you received and by being offended. As often as we are reminded that Satan is after the seed (Word of God), we are still surprised when things happen because of the Word. Remember, the word that God gave Joseph in his dream? His biological brothers hated him because of his dream. That dream came from God and some- how just like Satan they thought that they could overturn it. When God gives us a word it cannot be overturned or stopped. Satan knows that so he sends tribulation and persecution or send us opportunity to get offended so that word would not live and grows and mature to give the harvest that was intended by God for us to have. See Joseph's brothers Genesis 37:8.

*Genesis 37:8 And his brethren said to him, Shalt thou indeed reign over us? or shalt thou indeed have dominion over us? And they hated him yet the more for his dreams, and for his words.*

We cannot let people cause us to reject what God has given us by refusing to get pass the tribulations and persecutions or by making a choice to get offended with people, organizations, places or things. The word of God is powerful, reliable and life changing and we should hold onto it with all the strength that we can muster up.

Joseph brothers even planned to kill him to stop the maturity of his seed.

***Genesis 37:20 Come now therefore, and let us slay him, and cast him into some pit, and we will say, Some evil beast hath devoured him: and we shall see what will become of his dreams.***

This is just one example of what you may have to endure in order to mature your seed and reap the harvest of that seed (word). You cannot receive your seed in stony places and still plan to reap the harvest of it. I remember one time that God gave me a word and I was so happy but Satan told me that God was not going to do it and I believed it. So many things were happening to me and I thought that God was doing some things. I did not know that God would never change His mind about the word that He gives you; there- fore I thought that it was God speaking to me and it was not. I said to myself "I thought that God was going to do that" and I reason that He was not and I gave up the word as if was some of the other things that I had lost. The word was not rooted. And when a plant is not rooted, it is very easy to pull it up. Therefore, the flimsy shovel of precaution, tribulation or offense can dig it up quickly.

**Matthew 13:22 He also that received seed among the thorns is he that heareth the word; and the care of this world, and the deceitfulness of riches, choke the word, and he becometh unfruitful.**

It is amazing to me that seed (the word you receive) can become fruitful and you can still lose it. I believe that one of the reasons that Jesus tells us not to carry any care is because of it causing our seed (His word) to become unfruitful. Jesus considers believers His responsibility and as our Lord, our King and as our God, He is able to carry every care that we may have. There is a way that our care must be presented to Him. But we are not supposed to carry it ourselves. Peter talks about that in 1Peter 5:6-7.

> *1 Peter 5:6-7 Humble yourselves therefore under the mighty hand of God, that he may exalt you in due time: 7 Casting all your care upon him; for he careth for you.*

Peter says here to cast all of our care upon Him. In addition, the deceitfulness of riches chokes the seed and it became unfruitful. Sometimes we get so comfortable with the great amount of external possessions and things that we think that we do not need anything else. Money and things are not the end for life. Some people that have more money than they can spend in a lifetime are very lonely, or unhappy or not in good health, or have absolutely no peace. When we think in our mind that money or things can give us these kinds of things, we have been deceived and that deception will choke the seed (word) that you reconceived. The word of God is more valuable than anything we could ever have or imagine.

There is one example of Good Ground in this passage. That is found in Matthew 13:23.

> *Matthew 13:23 But he that received seed into the good ground is he that heareth the word, and understandeth it; which also beareth fruit, and bringeth forth, some an hundredfold, some sixty, some thirty.*

According to this verse, all we have to do is receive the seed into good ground and we have good ground when we hear the word, understand it and it brings forth a harvest of a hundredfold, sixtyfold or thirtyfold. Getting a hundredfold for seed sown did not start here in Matt. 13:23. The first mention of it in the King James Version was when Isaac received it for the seed he sowed in Genesis 26:12.

*Genesis 26:12 Then Isaac sowed in that land, and received in the same year an hundredfold: and the LORD blessed him.*

This land was obviously good ground for Isaac. Following seed from Genesis to Revelation takes us on an amazing journey.

**The Kingdom of Heaven is like Seed**

Seed is very important in the demonstration of what the Kingdom of Heaven is like. Jesus spent a lot of time talking about the Kingdom of Heaven and giving parables explain- ing how the kingdom of heaven operates and what that looks like. Two of His most powerful parable explanations used seed as the focal point of explaining what to expect. That is very important.

Since we understand that the Kingdom is not taught much in some churches, we may have to do a study of the Kingdom in more detail fashion on our own, but for now let's take a look at some to the explanations that Jesus gave using seed to demonstrate the power and the operation of the Kingdom:

**Matthew 13:24-30** Another parable He set forth before them, saying, The kingdom of heaven is like a man who sowed good seed in his field. **25** But while he was sleeping, his enemy came and sowed also darnel (weeds resembling wheat) among the wheat, and went on his way. **26** So when the plants sprouted and formed grain, the darnel (weeds) appeared also. **27** And the servants of the owner came to him and said, Sir, did you not sow good seed in your field? Then how does it have darnel shoots in it? **28** He replied to them, An enemy has done this. The servants said to him, Then do you want us to go and weed them out?

**29** But he said, No, lest in gathering the wild wheat (weeds resembling wheat), you root up the [true] wheat along with it. **30** Let them grow together until the harvest; and at harvest time I will say to the reapers, Gather the darnel first and bind it in bundles to be burned, but gather the wheat into my granary. **AMP**

What does this mean? The kingdom of heaven is like a man who sowed good seed (wheat) in his field and an enemy sowed bad seed and they both came up in his field. And when them both came up, a servant of the owner asked him, didn't you sow good seed, then why did the bad seed come up. The owner said an enemy has done this then the servant wanted to know if they should and weed out the bad seed, the owner answered no, let them grow together until harvest time and then bundle them together and burn them. To really understand let's find out how this happens in the natural.

## THE IMPORTANCE OF SEED

When you plant seed you have to first prepare the ground. You have to plow (till) it and depending on the nutrients in the soil you may have to add fertilizer. There are wild seeds in the soil that may have been deposited by the wind, animal dung or previous perennial plants, usually weeds, but not always. Even if the wild seed is on the top of the soil once you plow the ground you position all the seeds to grow. When the seed that you planted starts to grow you have to remove the weeds and all other plants that may interfere with the growth of each individual seedling that is coming up from the seed that you planted. However, sometimes the weeds or other plants come up so close to the seedling that it is impossible to pull it up without also pulling up the seedling that you planted. Sometimes the farmer will go ahead and pull that seedling up with the weeds in order to keep the weeds from choking out some of the other seedling. This way they only lose one instead two, three or even more.

The first spiritual truth in this parable is one is that of equal tolerance. The weed plant looks like the wheat plant. They look alike, but you can tell the difference so let them grow together until harvest time. Jesus does not want to risk the loss of one good seed trying to get rid of the bad ones. Good seed are the children of the kingdom. They are the seed of Jesus Christ and the bad seed are the children of Satan.

Remember that seed has its food and all that it is in it. It is going to reproduce after its own kind and so is the bad. But if you want the greatest harvest possible and God does, than you have to save all of the good seed. Once you gather your harvest of good seed you are ready to plant the next crop of good seed. Remember, we already said that the farmer always keep a remnant of the seed from the current crop to plant the crop in the next season.

Now, you say what is the spiritual truth that this applies to? The final harvest is when God takes His people with Him and send all of Satan's children to hell to be burned. This natural happening does explain a spiritual truth. I know by now you are wondering where this was mentioned in the Bible. Let's take a look at what Jesus had to say about this when He explained the spiritual meaning in Matthew 13:37-43.

***Matthew 13:37-43 37 He answered and said unto them, He that soweth the good seed is the Son of man; 38 The field is the world; the good seed are the children of the kingdom; but the tares are the children of the wicked one; 39 The enemy that sowed them is the devil; the harvest is the end of the world; and the reapers are the angels. 40 As therefore the tares are gathered and burned in the fire; so shall it be in the end of this world. 41 The Son of man shall send forth his angels, and they shall gather out of his kingdom all things that offend, and them which do iniquity; 42 And shall cast them into a furnace of fire: there shall be wailing and gnashing of teeth. 43 Then shall the righteous shine forth as the sun in the kingdom of their Father. Who hath ears to hear, let him hear.***

Now that we understand that **Jesus Christ is the sower, the field is the world, the good seed are the children of the kingdom, the enemy is the devil, tares are the children of the wicked one, the harvest is at the end of the world, the reapers are the angels** that Jesus will send, the tares (weeds- all things that offend and them which do iniquity) will be gathered and burned. That is going to be the end of this world. And the righteous shall shine forth as the sun in the kingdom of their Father. There is no wiggle room in this parable of how the kingdom of heaven is operation. Jesus wants those that belong to Him to understand that He will allow certain things to hap- pen just to save one person. Remember when Abraham was pleading with God for Sodom and Gomorrah and he stopped asking God when God said that He would save if for ten righteous people in Genesis 18:32.

**Genesis 18:32** *And he said, Oh let not the Lord be angry, and I will speak yet but this once: Peradventure ten shall be found there. And he said, I will not destroy it for ten's sake.*

Now we can see the heart of God in His kingdom, He will save one righteous person in the mist of things that offend and those which do iniquity, the children of the wicked one. This is one of the ways the Kingdom of Heaven operates. As much as some of us would like to get rid of some of the devils children they are not going anywhere. We do, however, have opportunity to offer them Jesus. They can be a part of the children of the kingdom if they say yes to the salvation that Jesus Christ offers all of us.

**Matthew 13:31-32** *Another parable put he forth unto them, saying, The kingdom of heaven is like to a grain of mustard seed, which a man took, and sowed in his field: 32 Which indeed is the least of all seeds: but when it is grown, it is the greatest among herbs, and becometh a tree, so that the birds of the air come and lodge in the branches therof.*

A grain of mustard is so small you can almost put it through an average needle's eye and you can put it through the eye of some of the larger needles. This is considered to be the smallest of all seeds; it is the greatest among herbs (vegetables) but when it is grown it become a tree large enough for birds to perch in the branches. How is it that you can plan an herb and get a tree? This is true of the mustard seed tree, but what is the spiritual truth. You can plant one word that seems to be so small into a person's life and it can grow into something unimaginable.

This was the kind of word that God gave Abraham concerning his seed. One small act of kindness can change the direction of a person's life. Most of the things that grow into something that grows to be extremely large started with a very small beginning. That is true for the body of Christ, which is true for businesses; even extremely large families start with just two people.

In the Kingdom of Heaven, we are not limited to what seem to be small beginnings. Remember, all that the seed need is in itself; therefore the mustard seed has all of that bigness in it. It is still an herb but it grows tall, it looks like a tree and it is strong enough for birds to nest in it. God kingdom is like that. One great example of this principle in the Old Testament is when God sent Elijah to help the widow woman that had decided that she was going to eat her last meal with her son and die in 1Kings 17:12.

> *1 Kings 17:12 And she said, As the LORD thy God liveth, I have not a cake, but an handful of meal in a barrel, and a little oil in a cruse: and, behold, I am gathering two sticks, that I may go in and dress it for me and my son, that we may*

> *eat it, and die. 13 And Elijah said unto her, Fear not; go and do as thou hast said: but make me thereof a little cake first, and bring it unto me, and after make for thee and for thy son. 14 For thus saith the LORD God of Israel, The barrel of meal shall not waste, neither shall the cruse of oil fail, until the day that the LORD sendeth rain upon the earth. 15 And she went and did according to the saying of Elijah: and she, and he, and her house, did eat many days. 16 And the barrel of meal wasted not, neither did the cruse of oil fail, according to the word of the LORD, which he spake by Elijah.*

Prophets and prophetic people today can still do this. Remember, you can plant one seed and get a multiplied harvest.

> *Mark 4:24-29 And he said unto them, Take heed what ye hear: with what measure ye mete, it shall be measured to you: and unto you that hear shall more be given. 25 For he that hath, to him shall be given: and he that hath not, from him shall be taken even that which he hath. 26 And he said, So is the kingdom of God, as if a man should cast seed into the ground; 27 And should sleep, and rise night and day, and the seed should spring and grow up, he knoweth not how. 28 For the earth bringeth forth fruit of herself; first the blade, then the ear, after that the full corn in the ear. 29 But when the fruit is brought forth, immediately he putteth in the sickle, because the harvest is come.*

The natural process of the growing of a seed of corn grows over a process of time. This may be a small challenge for those of us that are of the microwave generation. Jesus is explaining a kingdom of heaven principle. He starts by giving an illustration of hearing. When you study and meditate on what you hear, you will be given more than what you started with. This is something that we do sometimes with- out thinking about it. For instance, if we hear a word that we do not recognized and begin to wonder what it means, we will eventually look up the meaning. Once we do that, our knowledge based has increased and now we know much more than we did before. Sometimes we may be surprised because of the many definitions that we found and some- times we find that a particular word has several meaning. But if we do not look at it, some other thought that we have will kick it out and we lose all opportunity to add information to our vocabulary because we did not think about the word at all.

The word of God is like that also. Once you start to study the word of God, the Holy Spirit will help you understand what you are reading. Sometimes you may just think about in thought the verse that you are reading and all of a sudden you understand, not only do you understand, but you get additional revelation, more than you had expected. You can- not read the Bible as if you are reading a novel. If you try to do that, you will miss many great opportunities to grow in God. When you begin to grow in God, you don't know how or when that happens but somehow you know that you have grown and the things that use to give you a problem before is no longer an issue.

Jesus goes on to say that the kingdom of God is like a man planting seed into ground and going to sleep and rises night and day. This indicates a process of time. The seed that Jesus is talking about here is corn. The corn begins to grow but the sower does not know how this happens. Jesus goes on to say that the earth brings forth fruit of herself (we are the earth, the word is planted in our mind and we are to meditate on it until it gets into our hearts). The first thing that you see is the blade. Some of us give up when we see the blade because we do not realize that our crop is coming up and we settle for the blade. The next thing that we see is the ear, but we still do not have our crop, so it is not harvest time. Some of us go ahead and harvest the ear and never get the harvest that we were expecting. After that, we get the full corn in the ear. This is the fruit, it is finally here and now it is time to cut it because the harvest has come. You have to understand this principle, because if you do not you will give up and quit believing, or you execute a premature harvest. I remember one year I planted a garden in our back yard. One of the things that I planted was turnip greens. I planted a very long row of greens. I planted seed, so I was expecting to see the seedling first and then I knew that I had to wait six to eight weeks to get the full harvest.

My husband did not know anything about gardening or farming so when he saw the seedlings, he thought that was the full plant. He went out and executed a premature harvest pulled them all up and brought them in for me to cook. I was so disappointed because I knew that it was too late to start over and I would not get the harvest of that crop that particular year. How do we execute a premature harvest in the spirit?

One example is this: Let's say that we want a particular car, but it cost more than our budget can support right now. We need a car for transportation but we want a particular one. The way the kingdom of God works is that God will prepare that harvest for us but we have to go through the process of increasing our income in order to support our choice of vehicle. In order to increase our income, we may need to be better stewards of our money. We may not know that but God does. God begins to move us in the right direction but He knows that we need transportation. We get the opportunity to get a vehicle but it is not the one we wanted. Immediately, we settle for this one because we do not understand how the kingdom of heaven works. We say things like God did not want me to have that one, when in fact that was the blade. We may upgrade to one more car before we get the one that we wanted and if that happens that was the corn. And finally when we are able to get what we really wanted, the desire of our heart. Now we have the full corn in the ear and it is harvest time.

We are still talking about the importance of seed. God has put something inside of the seed and in the earth that cause things to grow and we know not how, but it works every time.

**Family Continue by Seed**

This is also interesting, because when you look at the specific of kinsman redeemer in the scripture you understand what God had in mind. In Matthew chapter 22, the Sadducees came to Jesus and tried to trick him because they wanted to prove that there is not resurrection. They used the kinsman redeemer law to try to prove a point in Matthew 22:23-29.

> *Matthew 22:23-29 The same day came to him the Sadducees, which say that there is no resurrection, and asked him, 24 Saying, Master, Moses said, If a man die, having no children, his brother shall marry his wife, and raise up seed*

*unto his brother. Mat 22:25 Now there were with us seven brethren: and the first, when he had married a wife, deceased, and, having no issue, left his wife unto his brother: 26 Likewise the second also, and the third, unto the seventh. 27 And last of all the woman died also. 28 Therefore in the resurrection whose wife shall she be of the seven? for they all had her.29 Jesus answered and said unto them, Ye do err, not knowing the scriptures, nor the power of God. 30 For in the resurrection they neither marry, nor are given in marriage, but are as the angels of God in heaven.*

The Sadducees were very much aware that God did not want a family name to be lost but that was not what they were trying to prove. They did not know that Jesus would become our kinsman redeemer. The important things to remember here is that God did not want the family name which was passed on through the male seed to be lost. We see that in Deuteronomy 25:5-10.

*Deuteronomy 25:5-10 If brothers are living together and one of them dies without a son, his widow must not marry outside the family. Her husband's brother shall take her and marry her and fulfill the duty of a brother-in-law to her. 6 The first son she bears shall carry on the name of the dead brother so that his name will not be blotted out from Israel. 7 However, if a man does not want to marry his brother's wife, she shall go to the elders at the town gate and say, "My husband's brother refuses to carry on his brother's name in Israel. He will not fulfill the duty of a brother-in-law to me." 8 Then the elders of his town shall summon him and talk to*

> *him. If he persists in saying, "I do not want to marry her," 9 his brother's widow shall go up to him in the presence of the elders, take off one of his sandals, spit in his face and say, "This is what is done to the man who will not build up his brother's family line." 10 That man's line shall be known in Israel as The Family of the Unsandaled. NIV*

Jesus is our kinsman and Christ is our Redeemer; therefore the seed that Jesus needed as Kinsman was passed down to Him as our brother. He is the first born of the family of God and had the responsibility to redeem us from the curse of the law and present us faultless into the family of God. As a result, we can go boldly to the throne of God as His sons. The curse of the law kept us from being able to do that because we could never meet the requirements of not committing any sin from the day of our conception in our mother's womb until the day we left the planet earth. We were in bondage under this world system and we needed a pure seed. We needed a seed that was not corrupt and need a clean seed that would allow us to come to God and to be in His presence without having to meet the requirements. Our brother the first Adam had died without passing down a pure seed. When he sinned they died. This is a death that forfeited the presence of God and fellowship with Him because that required a faultless state of being. The Apostle Paul talks about the seed that was in our brother Jesus Christ, our kinsman redeemer in Acts 13:22-23.

> *Acts 13:22-23 And when he had removed him, he raised up unto them David to be their king; to whom also he gave testimony, and said, I have found David the son of Jesse, a man after mine own heart, which shall fulfil all my will 23 Of*

*this man's seed hath God according to his promise raised unto Israel a Saviour, Jesus:*

It is through Jesus that we are born in the family of God and it is through Him that we have been given the power to become mature sons of God. This is a clear indication that He is our brother and that He has redeemed us. John talks about this in John 1:12-13.

*John 1:12-13 But as many as received him, to them gave he power to become the sons of God, even to them that believe on his name: 13 Which were born, not of blood, nor of the will of the flesh, nor of the will of man, but of God.*

Paul further explains this to the Galatians in Galatians 4:3-5.

*Galatians 4:3-5 Even so we, when we were children, were in bondage under the elements of the world: 4 But when the fulness of the time was come, God sent forth his Son, made of a woman, made under the law, 5 To redeem them that were under the law, that we might receive the adoption of sons.*

We needed a savior to put us back into faultless position with God. A kinsman redeemer was what we needed some- one that would give us His seed so that we could become the sons of God again and not be estranged from Him. That is truly how important it is to have the right seed. As we have found out, seed reproduces after its own kind. So it does not have to be good seed, it can be bad seed. We do not know what is in the seed that is transferred down from generation to generation. But God does because He is the one who set the system in place.

Jesus was the flesh part that qualified as our brother and Christ was the God part that qualified as our redeemer. We can see all of this operating through David's seed in Romans 1:3.

***Romans 1:3 Concerning his Son Jesus Christ our Lord, which was made of the seed of David according to the flesh;***

And through Abraham's seed in Romans 4:13-16.

***Romans 4:13-16 For the promise, that he should be the heir of the world, was not to Abraham, or <u>to his seed</u>, through the law, but through the righteousness of faith. 14 For if they which are of the law be heirs, faith is made void, and the promise made of none effect: 15 Because the law worketh wrath: for where no law is, there is no transgression. 16 Therefore it is of faith, that it might be by grace; to the end the promise might be sure to all the seed; not to that only which is of the law, but to that also which is of the faith of Abraham; who is the father of us all,***

## Chapter 10

## The Seed of the Covenant

God has given us His seed again through His only begotten Son. We are justified because of the sacrifice of Jesus to come into the family of God where there is not sin and because of this we have inherent seed that cannot be taint- ed, there is mothering that can change the holiness and righteousness of the seed of Jesus. Satan cannot accused it of any unrighteous act; therefore, we have a permanent position with God that always produces good seed. This seed cannot be changed because we did not earn it. Therefore we cannot change it by doing something or not doing something. It cannot be lost, we cannot lose it because we miss the mark (sin) because the price had be paid by Jesus for all sin past, present and future. And all we have to do is repent (turn from that) and God will forgive us and keep us in right standing with Him.

God gives covenant seed to those that He loves and He will let you know what kind of seed it is. You may not see the manifestation of it in your lifetime but if you believe that you have received it that is what God wants to happen. I am talk- ing about covenant seed to the believers. But I believe an example in the Old Testament will make some of this a little clearer later. Look at this example in Numbers 25:11-13.

*Numbers 25:11-13 Phinehas, the son of Eleazar, the son of Aaron the priest, hath turned my wrath away from the children of Israel, while he was zealous for my sake among them, that I consumed not the children of Israel in my jealousy. 12 Wherefore say, Behold, I give unto him my covenant of peace: 13 And he shall have it, and his seed after him, even the covenant of an everlasting priesthood; because he was zealous for his God, and made an atonement for the children of Israel.*

This is exciting to me because God is giving a seed covenant of peace and a seed of an everlasting priesthood to Phinehas. God said that he shall have it and his seed after him, therefore this is going to pass down through his blood-line. The future generations may not know when they have the favor of this seed manifesting in their lives. Whoever received that from Phinehas's bloodline may have just taken their life situations for granted. The Bible did not say one way or the other, but I can imagine God doing that on a regular basis and we not be aware of it because we don't understand seed. We don't pass that information down to our descendants. Some years ago I gave an offering to my spiritual father and his wife. This was not unusual because I was always looking for something to give them. This time however, for whatever reason only God knows, God spoke to me and said that because of that gift I would always have someone in my family to serve Him. That was a seed given to my bloodline. He did not say everybody, that lets me know that He is going to pick the person (grown) that He is going to plant that seed in my bloodline and it is going to travel from generation to generation.

Through the seed of Jesus Christ God has position us to win every battle, to be His sons and to be the bride of His son, Jesus Christ. As His sons we have the power and authority to give to others what He has given to us and as

His wife we are positioned to receive all we need and want from Him. We can ask Jehovah God our Father anything according to His word in the name of Jesus and it be given us. As His wife God gives to us what we need personally from Him. As His sons He gives through us to others. As believers in the Lord Jesus Christ, we have access to the fullness of the Godhead.

I was saved as a child but when I was a child in the natural I did not think much about this at all. Then when I became an adult believer I decided to backslide. For many years the Lord tugged on me to come back and one day I said yes. When that happened I begin to study the word of God and I found out something astounding. There was no power in the churches that I knew about. It seem to me to be a twice a week social event. Sunday service and bible study one night a week. We also had revivals and different department (usher, choir, etc.) anniversaries, including the church and pastors anniversaries. But nothing was happening that Jesus or His disciples said should be happening.

We prayed for the sick but I do not remember any of them being healed instantly. We said maybe Jesus will do it or maybe He won't but anyway. He is God He can do what He wants. And if He does not want us to be healed, we will not be healed. I was pondering about this and I wondered what had happened to our ability to do sign, wonders or miracles and why we as believers could not speak to a fig tree and tell it what to do and it be done. Some Christians were cast- ing out demons that were really works of the flesh and at that time I did not even know the difference. I was thinking something is wrong. We were singing songs like I beat the Devil running and I am so glad. Should we be running from the Devil, if he is a spirit how can you run faster? I did not see anything in the word of God about running from the Devil but I sang the song because I was looking for an excuse not to obey God. Whatever I saw the saints do I reason that it was good because that was easier to do than to obey what the Bible said to do. I cannot say why it was like that because today I don't know the answer. I just know that I could not find the answers that I sought. Sometime later, I heard about some miraculous things that some churches were doing in other cities and even in other countries but I did not get to see any of that personally.

As a result of my hunger to know what happened, God sent people to me and put me in situations and even churches that were doing some part of what the Bible said we should be doing and that was what I was looking for. Then the Holy Spirit begin to train me Himself about some things were happening and why some things were not happening. Being the big baby in Christ that I was at that time I was happy with what information and revelation that was given me and I quit asking so many questions. However, He kept growing me up in Him until I begin to realize that the word of God was the same and nothing had changed. I found out that the word of God is as reverent for today. One of the areas in the word of God that I specifically remember is "Faith." The word of God says that it is impossible to please God with- out faith, but I did not know what that looked like. Therefore, when I operated in faith in my ignorance, I took the credit and said it was my education or my intellect but it was all me I did not give God any credit. I have to admit faith was mentioned in church as something we should do but I did not see anyone living a life of faith or even claim- ing that God had honored their faith. God gave us the example of Abraham to let us know that we can get impossible things done by faith.

I said all of that to say this we do not know what seed we have in us as children of God. We have not tapped into the vast treasure of seed that we have in Christ. We for the most part do not expect to harvest the seed that God has put there for one reason or another but nevertheless the seed is there. Jesus said that we that believed on Him would not only do what He did but we would do greater works than He did.

*John 14:12 Verily, verily, I say unto you, He that believeth on me, the works that I do shall he do also; and greater works than these shall he do; because I go unto my Father.*

If you are reading this, have you done some of the things that He did, if so, have you done greater? I know that I have not and I have a long way to go but I want to purpose in my heart to do what Jesus said I could do. What did He do and why does He expect greater. Let's look at what He did first because all of that seed is in us. We know that He expects greater because we have God the Holy Spirit in us to help us do it all.

What are some examples of seed that believers have working in them?

- We are the sons of God.

*Romans 8:14 For as many as are led by the Spirit of God, they are the sons of God.*

We have already discussed being born into the family of God in John 1:12. Now we see that we must also be led by the Spirit of God. When we are led by the Spirit of God nothing is impossible for us. Nothing and no one can stop us from doing what called us to do because no one is greater than God. In this same passage we are giving the under- standing of being the children and adopted into the family of God and if we are His children then we should manifest in the earth what He manifest in the universe. Here is what was said about that in Romans 8:15-31.

> *Romans 8:15-21 For [the Spirit which] you have now received [is] not a spirit of slavery to put you once more in bondage to fear, but you have received the Spirit of adoption [the Spirit producing sonship] in [the bliss of] which we cry, Abba (Father)! Father! 16 The Spirit Himself [thus] testifies together with our own spirit, [assuring us] that we are children of God. 17 And if we are [His] children, then we are [His] heirs also: heirs of God and fellow heirs with Christ [sharing His inheritance with Him]; only we must share His suffering if we are to share His glory. 18 [But what of that?] For I consider that the sufferings of this present time (this present life) are not worth being com- pared with the glory that is about to be revealed to us and in us and [g]for us and [h]conferred on us! 19 For [even the whole] creation (all nature) waits expectantly and longs earnestly for God's sons to be made known [waits for the revealing, the dis- closing of their sonship]. 20 For the creation (nature) was subjected to [i]frailty (to futility, condemned to frustration), not because of some intentional fault on its part, but by the will of Him Who so subjected it—[yet] with the hope 21 That nature (creation) itself will be set free from its bondage to decay and corruption [and gain an entrance] into the glorious freedom of God's children.*

## THE IMPORTANCE OF SEED

*Romans 8:22-26 We know that the whole creation [of irrational creatures] has been moaning together in the pains of labor until now. 23 And not only the creation, but we ourselves too, who have and enjoy the first fruits of the [Holy] Spirit [a foretaste of the blissful things to come] groan inwardly as we wait for the redemption of our bodies [from sensuality and the grave, which will reveal] our adoption (our manifestation as God's sons). 24 For in [this] hope we were saved. But hope [the object of] which is seen is not hope. For how can one hope for what he already sees? 25 But if we hope for what is still unseen by us, we wait for it with patience and composure. 26 So too the [Holy] Spirit comes to our aid and bears us up in our weakness; for we do not know what prayer to offer nor how to offer it worthily as we ought, but the Spirit Himself goes to meet our supplication and pleads in our behalf with unspeakable yearnings and groanings too deep for utterance.*

*Romans 8:27-31 And He Who searches the hearts of men knows what is in the mind of the [Holy] Spirit [what His intent is], because the Spirit inter- cedes and pleads [before God] in behalf of the saints according to and in harmony with God's will. 28 We are assured and know that [[j]God being a partner in their labor] all things work together and are [fitting into a plan] for good to and for those who love God and are called accord- ing to [His] design and purpose. 29 For those whom He foreknew [of whom He was [k]aware and [l]loved beforehand], He also destined from the beginning [foreordaining them] to be molded into the image of His Son [and share inwardly His likeness], that He might become the firstborn among many brethren. 30 And those whom He thus foreordained, He also called; and those whom He called, He also justified (acquitted, made righteous, putting them into right standing with Himself). And those whom He justified, He also glorified [raising them to a heavenly dignity and condition or state of being]. 31 What then shall we say to [all] this? If God is for us, who [can be] against us? [Who can be our foe, if God is on our side?] AMP*

This is a long passage but it reflects what God has done for His sons. We are His children but we are first His creation. We are creatures of God's creation. He created us to be His sons. He put His seed in us and because of this nothing is impossible for us. When Adam was created male and female they were free of sin, there was not sin in them. God does not fellowship with sin; therefore they had to be sin free. Adam was able to name everything that God brought to him. He had no intelligence, intellect, education, prior knowledge of anything except what God had given to them. They freely fellowshipped with God without hindrance of any kind, but once sin was introduced to them they could no longer fellowship with God freely. God had to correct that situation because He loved them (us) His creations. He wants fellowship with us. Therefore He created a situation of salvation through Jesus Christ that cannot be changed.

The blood that was shed by Jesus was what positioned us to a permanent spot in the family of God and it cannot be moved, it cannot be stopped, and it cannot be compromised as was done to Adam and Eve in the Garden of Eden. God expects us to pray and ask for what we need to make things successful but He knew we did not know what to say. Remember words are seed, so He sent the Holy Spirit to help us with weakness, to our aid and bears us up in our weakness. For we do not know what prayer to offer nor how to offer it worthily as we ought, but the Spirit Himself goes to meet our supplication and pleads on our behalf with unspeakable yearnings and groanings too deep for utterance. And He searches the hearts of men knows what is in the mind of the Holy Spirit what His intent is, because the Spirit intercedes and pleads before God in behalf of the saints according to and in harmony with God's will.

In the beginning when God created Adam male and female created He them. There was no struggle to do what God said to do or to be where God said to be. Adam did not choose his place of residence; God placed him where he wanted him to be. They did not have no in their mouth to God nor did they think about things that were not of God. The seed that God had given them was holy and pure. There was no need to overcome sickness, rejection, intimidation, lust of the flesh or any of those things because that did not live in God's seed. All of that lives in the seed of Satan and Satan used the serpent to introduce that to them. So now God creature has to struggle through the process of becoming one with God without all of the bad seed passed down from the sin of Adam.

I can imagine that Adam became angry for the first time with the serpent. He had not been introduced to anger before because that seed did not live in him. But once he saw what he lost because of disobeying God his first reaction was to blame someone. He blamed the woman and the woman blamed the serpent. Blame did not live in them before. All of this behavior came from a bad seed, an unholy seed given to them by the serpent and they received that seed.

God did not leave it up to us to correct any of this, He did it all himself, He foreordained us, He also called; and those whom He called, He also justified (acquitted, made righteous, putting them into right standing with Himself). And those whom He justified, He also glorified [raising them to a heavenly dignity and condition or state of being]. This is interesting because many times we may be afraid that Satan will take our relationship with God away as he did Adam. But God fixed that also. God is for us and since God is for us, who can be against us? Who can be our foe, since God is on our side? We can take our position as His sons and do what Jesus did when He was here on earth. We can heal the sick, we can raise the dead, we can perform creative miracles, we can feed five thousand with a small amount of food, we can open blind eyes, we can cause the lame to walk again and much more if we avail ourselves as at the sons of God and mature in the ways and the things of God. These should be everyday common things for believers because it is all in the seed of Jesus Christ. God understood our fear of the serpent so he sent us a word (Jesus) who spoke about this.

> *Luke 10:18-19 And he said unto them, I beheld Satan as lightning fall from heaven. 19 Behold, I give unto you power to tread on serpents and scorpions, and over all the power of the enemy: and nothing shall by any means hurt you.*

Jesus said "I saw Satan fall from heaven" and I give you power over him, you can tread on serpents and scorpions and over all of the power of the enemy and nothing shall by any means hurt you. That is truly comforting if we believe it, but just in case you need more conformation He mentions in Mark 16:17-18.

*Mark 16:17-18 And these signs shall follow them that believe; In my name shall they cast out devils; they shall speak with new tongues; 18 They shall take up serpents; and if they drink any deadly thing, it shall not hurt them; they shall lay hands on the sick, and they shall recover.*

All of this should be common events among believers, but how many do you know that cast out devils or lay hands on the sick and they recover. Thank God for doctors because believers do not know who they are and they rarely even think about casting out devils and healing the sick. But Jesus said that this activity would be signs that follow them that believe. Then why do we not see more of the signs, it is because of fear. We must overcome fear and because we do not believe that God would give His sons that kind of power. Therefore, we never stir up our ground and activate the dormant seed that Jesus has left in His bloodline.

We must not mind the struggles and processes that we have to go through to be a mature son of God. To work with God no matter what comes our way to accomplish what He wants to accomplish in the earth and partner with God to accomplish the assignment that He sent us to the earth to do.

- We are the bride of Christ

> *John 3:29 He that hath the bride is the bridegroom: but the friend of the bridegroom, which standeth and heareth him, rejoiceth greatly because of the bridegroom's voice: this my joy therefore is fulfilled.*

As God's sons we get things from God to give to others but as His bride we get things that belong to us. Isaiah talks about this in Isaiah 62:4-8.

> *Isaiah 62:4-8 You [Judah] shall no more be termed Forsaken, nor shall your land be called Desolate any more. But you shall be called Hephzibah [My delight is in her], and your land be called Beulah [married]; for the Lord delights in you, and your land shall be married [owned and protected by the Lord]. 5 For as a young man marries a virgin [O Jerusalem], so shall your sons marry you; and as the bridegroom rejoices over the bride, so shall your God rejoice over you. 6 I have set watchmen upon your walls, O Jerusalem, who will never hold their peace day or night; you who [are His servants and by your prayers] put the Lord in remembrance [of His promises], keep not silence, 7 And give Him no rest until He establishes Jerusalem and makes her a praise in the earth. 8 The Lord has sworn by His right hand and by His mighty arm: Surely I will not again give your grain as food for your enemies, and [the invading sons of] aliens shall not drink your new wine for which you have toiled; AMP*

We are kings and lords

*1 Timothy 6:15 Which in his times he shall shew, [who is] the blessed and only Potentate, the King of kings, and Lord of lords;*

The Greek word for king, as it pertains to believers, is basileuō which means to be king, to exercise kingly power, to reign, of the governor of a province of the rule of the Messiah of the reign of Christians in the millennium metaph. to exercise the highest influence, to control. Jesus is the commander of the kings, He is the King of kings. The Greek word for His reign as King is basileus which means leader of the people, prince, commander, lord of the land, king. What does Jesus want us to reign over? He wants us to reign over the kingdoms of this world and take dominion over things that Satan had rule and reign over before He came. This is mentioned in Revelation 11:15.

*Revelation 11:15 And the seventh angel sounded; and there were great voices in heaven, saying, The kingdoms of this world are become the kingdoms of our Lord, and of his Christ; and he shall reign for ever and ever.*

There are seven of these kingdoms and they are: business, government, media, arts and entertainment, education, the family and religion. These are the things that influence our society and our way of life and Jesus wants us to rule and reign over them. There are also called mountains.

God owns the earth and He wants His people to manage the earth, because he has given us that power. We see our direction to move these mountains in Mark 11:23.

> *Mark 11:23 For verily I say unto you, That whoso- ever shall say unto this mountain, Be thou removed, and be thou cast into the sea; and shall not doubt in his heart, but shall believe that those things which he saith shall come to pass; he shall have whatsoever he saith.*

If you think that too many evil things are happening in our society that means that some believers have not taken over a particular kingdom to the point where Christ reigns and is seen in the health and wealth of that kingdom as it pertains to the things of God.

The word lord as it pertains to man in this passage is the Greek word lord kyrieuō which means to be lord of, to rule, have dominion over of things and forces, to exercise influence upon, to have power over. Jesus has given us the authority to have dominion and power over things and forces. He can do that because God owns everything and He is lord over it all. The Greek meaning for the word Lord as it pertains to Jesus is kyrios which means he to whom a per- son or thing belongs, about which he has power of deciding; master, lord, the possessor and disposer of a thing, the owner; one who has control of the person, the master, in the state: the sovereign, prince, chief, the Roman emperor, is a title of honour expressive of respect and reverence, with which servants greet their master, this title is given to: God, the Messiah.

We are a chosen generation - royal priesthood - a holy nation and a peculiar people

> *1 Peter 2:9-17 But ye are a covering, veil; that ye should shew forth the praises of him who hath called you out of darkness into his marvellous light: 10 Which in time past were not a people,*

*but are now the people of God: which had not obtained mercy, but now have obtained mercy. 11 Dearly beloved, I beseech you as strangers and pilgrims, abstain from fleshly lusts, which war against the soul; 12 Having your conversation honest among the Gentiles: that, whereas they speak against you as evildoers, they may by your good works, which they shall behold, glorify God in the day of visitation. 13 Submit yourselves to every ordinance of man for the Lord's sake: whether it be to the king, as supreme; 14 Or unto governors, as unto them that are sent by him for the punishment of evildoers, and for the praise of them that do well. 15 For so is the will of God, that with well doing ye may put to silence the ignorance of foolish men: 16 As free, and not using your liberty for a cloke of maliciousness, but as the servants of God. 17 Honour all men. Love the brotherhood. Fear God. Honour the king.*

Believers are a chosen generation, a royal priesthood and a holy nation. This passage gives us specific information about the fact that God has called and chosen us and made us a holy nation able to produce and reproduce holy seed. Peter explains here that we were once not people of God but God has changed all of that and with that comes some responsibilities. One such responsibility is to abstain from fleshly lusts which wars against us. Can you imagine fellowshipping with seed that the crop of which will bring us into a state of warring against ourselves? In addition, we have to live a life that will cause people to see the glory of God. We get clear directions of what is in our seed and what is expected of each one of us. We must not position our- selves as evildoers, so that people will not speak against us but they may by our good works, which they see, glorify God in the day of visitation. We must submit ourselves to every ordinance of man, not just the ones we like but all of them for the Lord's sake: whether it be to the king (our boss), as supreme (the legal system, police, court etc.) unto governors, (elected officials), as unto them that are sent by him for the punishment of evildoers, and for the praise of them that do well. God is expecting us to do well; He is not expecting that any of these systems should harm us. For so is the will of God, that with well doing ye may put to silence the ignorance of foolish men. We are free, but we are not to use our liberty as a covering or veil of maliciousness, but as the servants of God. We are to honor all men, love the brotherhood, fear God and honor the king. It is all in the holy seed of a chosen generation - royal priesthood - a holy nation and a peculiar people.

Peter is telling us what lives in the holy seed and what does not. He explains that all that is in the holy seed is light and all of the other is darkness. We are children of the light because God had called us out of darkness into His marvelous light and none of things that we are to abstain from lives in God.

Before we can get to this wonderful holy state of being Peter tells us all about the process that we must successfully complete in 1 Peter 2:1-8.

> *1 Peter 2:1-8 Wherefore laying aside all malice, and all guile, and hypocrisies, and envies, and all evil speakings, 2 As newborn babes, desire the sincere milk of the word, that ye may grow thereby: 3 If so be ye have tasted that the Lord is gracious. 4 To whom coming, as unto a living stone, disallowed indeed of men, but chosen of*

> *God, and precious, 5 Ye also, as lively stones, are built up a spiritual house, an holy priesthood, to offer up spiritual sacrifices, acceptable to God by Jesus Christ. 6 Wherefore also it is contained in the scripture, Behold, I lay in Sion a chief corner stone, elect, precious: and he that believeth on him shall not be confounded. 7 Unto you therefore which believe he is precious: but unto them which be disobedient, the stone which the builders disallowed, the same is made the head of the corner, 8 And a stone of stumbling, and a rock of offence, even to them which stumble at the word, being dis- obedient: whereunto also they were appointed.*

Our bodies as believers are the house of God; as such we are a holy priesthood able to off up spiritual sacrifices accept- able to God by Jesus Christ. Now the words sacrifice in the Greek is isthysia meaning a sacrifice, victim.

According to on line dictionary merriam-webster.com the word victim means a person who has been attacked, injured, robbed, or killed by someone else, a person who is cheated or fooled by someone else, someone or something that is harmed by an unpleasant event (such as an illness or accident). This is not seemingly a pleasant situation, but it is a safe one according to the word of God. Our spirit man will always choose to make us the sacrifice because Jesus was our sacrifice and that is where we can tap into the holy seed. Notice in verse 1 Peter talks about laying aside all of the bad seed, he said lay aside all malice, the word malice in the Greek is *kakia* meaning - malignity, malice, ill-will, desire to injure wickedness, depravity, wickedness that is not ashamed to break laws, evil, trouble. This is really bad seed and you and I do not want to raise this kind of crop in our lives.

It is difficult if you do not understand the sowing and reap- ing because people will do things that may cause you to want to have ill will toward them or the desire to injure them but we must resist that and lay that seed aside. Peter included all guile the Greek word for guile is ***dolos*** which means craft, deceit and guile, and all hypocrisies. The Greek word for hypocrisies is ***hypokrisis*** which means an answering, an answer, the acting of a stage player, dissimulation, or hypocrisy, and all envies, and all evil speakings. The Greek word for this is katalalia which means defamation, evil speaking, backbitting. All of these are actions that come from Satan and we do not want to plant any of these seeds. These are things(seeds) that baby Christians may have in their system but they must lay them aside and have the desire to feed on the sincere milk of the word, that ye may grow thereby and as you grow you will have tasted that the Lord is gracious. Men will not approve of what you are doing but you are chosen of God, and precious.

**The Entry Gates of Seed**

By now you may be asking how to stop collecting bad seed or how do I protect my holy seed. There are many ways for seed that you don't want to sneak into our ground. Three of the major ways are 1. television, DVD, internet and other vision electronics (eye gate), 2. radio, CD's and other audio electronic devices (ear gate) and 3. associations with, people, places and things. We have to be careful about what we see, hear and do. Some things may seem innocent but we have to examine the spirit behind it. We have already mentioned the behaviors to avoid in previous chapters, however, we cannot fellowship with things without them becoming a seed for us.

For instance, if you watch television shows where there is envy, evil speaking, and backbiting etc., you are inviting those seeds into your ground. If you have friends that do not celebrate God and do not want you to do it, you invite those seeds into your ground. It does not matter if these are long- time friends or recent, you cannot allow them to draw you into things like malice and guile. If you fellowship with people that frequently use foul language, you will one day find yourself saying one or more of those words and then you say where did that come from. It came from the seed that snuck in while you were not paying attention to your surroundings or the company that you keep. Likewise, you can plant good seed in your ground by obeying the word of God and receiving the seed that God has already passed down from our Lord Jesus Christ. It is possible to do everything that God said that we could do. It is possible to be everything that God said that we can be. It is possible because we are exactly who God said that we are. God is not concerned about our nationality or social status. He created us in His image and as His likeness and that is what He is concerned about.

We are the object of God's love. He created us to love us and for us to love Him. He wants to spend time with us and be a vital part of our lives. Satan did not create us but he too want to be a vital part of our lives. He wants to try to make the word of God null and void but that is impossible. However, it is possible for him to offer us bad seeds so that we spend more time with him than God. He is constantly crouching at our door waiting for us to invite him in. The best example of this is the story of Cain and Abel the sons of Adam and Eve after they sinned. That seed of sin was received by Cain from his parents, yet God was not willing that he be lost and separated from Him. Because you cannot be with God in an intimate way if you love to fellowship with sin more than being in the presence of God.

> *Genesis 4:6-8 And the LORD said unto Cain, Why art thou wroth? and why is thy countenance fallen? 7 If thou doest well, shalt thou not be accepted? and if thou doest not well, sin lieth at the door. And unto thee shall be his desire, and thou shalt rule over him. 8 And Cain talked with Abel his brother: and it came to pass, when they were in the field, that Cain rose up against Abel his brother, and slew him.*

Cain was envious of his brother because God accepted his brother Abel's offering and did not accept him. The seed of envy was present in Cain. He did not want to give God the best of what he had, but that is what his brother Abel did. He wanted God to bless him but he did not want to bless God. This will let you know how tinder God's heart toward Cain because God knew what Cain did but He gave him a chance to bring a better offering. When God saw that sad look on Cain's face he asked him why are you wroth, why has you countenance fallen? If you do well I will accept it, but Cain wanted God to accept his sin and God will never do that. So his next move was to kill his brother. As that seed grew in Cain it begins to rule over him and he did not even know that what he was doing would banish him from the presence of God forever.

> *Genesis 4:14-15 Behold, thou hast driven me out this day from the face of the earth; and from thy face shall I be hid; and I shall be a fugitive and*

*a vagabond in the earth; and it shall come to pass, that every one that findeth me shall slay me. 15 And the LORD said unto him, Therefore whosoever slayeth Cain, vengeance shall be taken on him sevenfold. And the LORD set a mark upon Cain, lest any finding him should kill him.*

When Cain cried out to God, he was able to get what he requested from God, but he was not allowed to stay in God's presence or with the people of God. Not only that but because he would not repent of his sin even of killing his brother Abel. It was passed on to his children as an iniquity and became a generational curse. His son did what he did and more and his son did not start the curse but he is going to pass it on to children generations down the road.

Take a look at this tragic story of Cain's grandson.

*Genesis 4:16-24 And Cain went out from the presence of the LORD, and dwelt in the land of Nod, on the east of Eden. 17 And Cain knew his wife; and she conceived, and bare Enoch: and he build- ed a city, and called the name of the city, after the name of his son, Enoch. 18 And unto Enoch was born Irad: and Irad begat Mehujael: and Mehujael begat Methusael: and Methusael begat Lamech. 19 And Lamech took unto him two wives: the name of the one was Adah, and the name of the other Zillah. 20 And Adah bare Jabal: he was the father of such as dwell in tents, and of such as have cattle. And his brother's name was Jubal: he was the father of all such as handle the harp and organ. 22 And Zillah, she also bare Tubalcain, an*

> *instructer of every artificer in brass and iron: and the sister of Tubalcain was Naamah. 23 And Lamech said unto his wives, Adah and Zillah, Hear my voice; ye wives of Lamech, hearken unto my speech: for I have slain a man to my wounding, and a young man to my hurt. 24 If Cain shall be avenged sevenfold, truly Lamech seventy and sevenfold. This is tragic because Lamech is not Cain's son or even his great grandson; this bad seed of murder was passed down generations to him.*

Notice what he said. "I have slain a man to my wounding and a young man to my hurt, if Cain shall be avenged sevenfold, truly Lamech seventy and sevenfold." I can imagine that Cain never dreamed that what he did would ever go any further than him. What is even more tragic is when Lamech started the practice of having more than one wife. See how seed grows! All Cain had to do in the very beginning when he brought an incorrect offering was to correct his offering, obey God and do well and God would have accepted that.

**The Fullness of the Godhead**

Believers have the fullness of the Godhead in them through Christ. The Holy Spirit is the agent of that access. We can do all that God the Father does as we have seen in the scriptures. We can do all that the Son (Jesus Christ) did as we have seen in the scriptures. We can do all that the Holy Spirit did as we have seen in the scriptures. That is some- times difficult for us to imagine since we have so much in us that does not seem like God. But the seed of the Godhead is what we have that allows us to do all that they have demonstrated to us and more. Nothing is impossible for God. Yet believers operate as if ninety percent of what they need to do is too hard for God or they think that He will not do that for them.

We depend on the world system for so much, rather than God. We trust banks and other financial institutions to loan us money but we will not have faith in God to give us the money. God is the source of the banks yet we trust them more. We trust doctors to heal us but we will not believe God for healing. I remember a prophetic word that God gave Bishop Walker a few years back for the body of Christ. God said that He was going to cause tremendous medical breakthroughs to happen because He wanted his people healed. They did not have the faith to believer Him for heal- ing. Sometime ago I was talking to a friend and she was telling me how see kept praying to God about her back pain. However, she never asked Him to heal it. She never asked Him to stop the pain and she said that God told her to go to the doctor. WOW! God knew that she did not have the faith to get the healing that He had already provided over two thousand years ago, so He told her the next best thing, go to the doctor.

We will believe intellectual people more often than we will believe God because some of them like for everything to make sense. The way God does things do not make sense and because of that we allow people to talk us out of believing God. We let tradition keep us from believing God and operation in the power that He has given us. We let Satan lie and deceive us because we do not trust God, we have to trust God even when we have no idea how or why some- thing that He said would happen. It is in and through Jesus Christ that we are victorious in everything. There is nothing lacking that we need and nothing missing that we need. There is nothing on this planet that has the power to stop what God has done for us. Paul explains this in Colossians 2:8-10.

> *Colossians 2:8-10 Beware lest any man spoil you through philosophy and vain deceit, after the tradition of men, after the rudiments of the world, and not after Christ. 9 For in him dwelleth all the fulness of the Godhead bodily. 10 And ye are complete in him, which is the head of all principality and power:*

Remember, God system does not make sense sometimes and we have to just step out on faith. God's financial system is like that. There are so many components of God's financial system that are baffling to those that try through their intellect to explain what happens. For instance God will ask you to give your last and that become the first of a long stream of income. That is the principle of the First Fruit Offering. It does not make sense for your last to also be your first.

Since we have to deal with all of these issues that cause us not to trust God or His system we have to change our minds and let the mind of Christ Jesus be in us. As mentioned in Philippians 2:5-9.

> *Philippians 2:5-9 Let this mind be in you, which was also in Christ Jesus: 6 Who, being in the form of God, thought it not robbery to be equal with God: 7 But made himself of no reputation, and took upon him the form of a servant, and was made in the likeness of men: 8 And being found in fashion as a man, he humbled himself, and became obedient unto death, even the death of the cross. 9 Wherefore God also hath highly exalted him, and given him a name which is*

*above every name: 10 That at the name of Jesus every knee should bow, of things in heaven, and things in earth, and things under the earth;*

We have to think it not robbery to be made in image and likeness of God. Jesus has said that we can use his name as the bride of Christ and we know if we do that every knee should bow. Let us begin to walk in the fullness of the Godhead in our everyday lives. God helps me do any and everything that I ask Him. Nothing is too small or too large.

I ask him when I go in the grocery store to help be stay within the budget that I have to spend. I did not know that He would do that at first but then He begin to impress on me what to put in the basket and what not to and when I got to the register to pay for it the bill would be with 1 or 2 cents of what I had to spend and sometimes it would be exactly. That is just one of many examples. God want to be a part of everything that we do. However, some things that we do we do not want Him to be a part of because we know that He will not sanction that particular thing because it is sin or attached to sin.

The seed we plant will always yield a harvest, therefore we have to plan our next season with the careful planting of seed. We have talked much about seed but let us be practical of what can come to us. If you give away a car, that is a seed and someone will give you a car or you will get one without cost or even without requesting one from God. If you pay someone cell phone bill so that they can have it because you know they can't and they need if for emergencies etc., that is a seed and you will get a return crop on that. If you offer kindness to someone, that is a seed and some- one will be kind to you. It may be a person, it may be a businesses, it may be an organization etc., but the harvest of the seed is come you are going to get a harvest from that. If you are mean and nasty to someone, that is a seed and that harvest is surely coming in due season. If you are sarcastic in your communication to people and you hurt someone in the process, you will surely see the maturity of that seed in a coming season, it will not necessary be a return of sarcasm, because the seed was hurt and pain, some synonyms for sarcasm are scorn, ridicule and contempt, your crop may come up in one of these. If you lie, that is a seed and people or different groups (businesses, governments etc.) will lie to you because the harvest is coming. If you cheat, that is a seed, If you steal, that is a seed, if you fornicate that is a seed. Whatever sin you commit is seed and at the end of that matter is death in that particular matter. It is just a matter to the time it takes for the seed to grow and produce more seed and what that happens you experience the harvest.

God does not want us to sin. He knows the results of those seeds and He has protected those that are His from the crop of all of that because He has given us a holy seed through Jesus Christ. We are able to stop planting those kinds of seed with His help if it is our will to do so. All of this is explained in Romans, let us look at the process of how Jesus did this in Romans 6:10-21.

> *Romans 6:10-21 For in that he died, he died unto sin once: but in that he liveth, he liveth unto God. 11 Likewise reckon ye also yourselves to be dead indeed unto sin, but alive unto God through Jesus Christ our Lord. 12 Let not sin therefore reign in your mortal body, that ye should obey it in the lusts thereof. 13 Neither yield ye your members as instruments of*

# THE IMPORTANCE OF SEED

*unrighteousness unto sin: but yield yourselves unto God, as those that are alive from the dead, and your members as instruments of righteousness unto God. 14 For sin shall not have dominion over you: for ye are not under the law, but under grace. 15 What then? shall we sin, because we are not under the law, but under grace? God forbid. 16 Know ye not, that to whom ye yield yourselves servants to obey, his servants ye are to whom ye obey; whether of sin unto death, or of obedience unto righteousness? 17 But God be thanked, that ye were the servants of sin, but ye have obeyed from the heart that form of doctrine which was delivered you. 18 Being then made free from sin, ye became the servants of righteousness. 19 I speak after the manner of men because of the infirmity of your flesh: for as ye have yielded your members servants to uncleanness and to iniquity unto iniquity; even so now yield your members servants to righteousness unto holiness. 20 For when ye were the servants of sin, ye were free from righteousness. 21 What fruit had ye then in those things whereof ye are now ashamed? for the end of those things is death.*

As this passage says in verse 21, the result is fruit. You determine what fruit you want to produce because it will have plenty of seed. Remember, it all begins with one seed.

God wants us to plants seeds of righteousness. The Greek word for righteousness in this passage is dikaiosynē and it means - in a broad sense: state of him who is as he ought to be, righteousness, the condition acceptable to God, the doc- trine concerning the way in which man may attain a state approved of God, integrity, virtue, purity of life, rightness, correctness of thinking feeling, and acting in a narrower sense, justice or the virtue which gives each his due. Remember Cain? We do not want to make the decision that he made to plant seed that will separate us from God.

Let us move forward in the things of God and turn everything over to Him, every care, every hope, every trust, every dream and every assignment. God's righteousness is full of light and life. There is no turning in God; it is always going to be like this. There are things that we know to do but we have not decided to do them. One example is living by faith. Believers live by faith not by signs, wonders and miracles, those are for unbelievers. Since we know that it is impossible to please God without faith let us move forward in faith. Let us plant seeds of faith. Another example is giving God the tithe. We know that we should do that but we don't know how devastating it is not to tithe. If you do not tithe, that is a seed and from that you get a harvest of a curse with a curse. Another thing to remember regarding the tithe and offering, is tithe belongs to God. It is not an offering to God since it belongs to Him. If the offering is money it is seed also. You get a harvest from your offering; therefore if your seed is money your harvest is money. Your offering may be something like a house. Then the house becomes seed and your harvest will be a house. Another example is that of dis- obeying a specific direct order from God not to do something.

***1 Chronicles 16:21-22 He suffered no man to do them wrong: yea, he reproved kings for their sakes, 22 Saying, Touch not mine anointed, and do my prophets no harm.***

God said here touch not His anointed. There are no conditions under which you can do this and make God like it. If you do, it is a seed and you are going to get the harvest. Even if it is your spouse, your child, your mother, your brother or anyone. Because if they are in Christ chances are they are at least His anointed. Especially if they are already committed and operation in ministry of the Lord Jesus Christ. When we understand that everything that we do, say or think is seed, we will become a better manager and a better steward of our tomorrows.

Most people do not recognize their harvest when it comes. They are puzzled about some of the things that show up in their lives. We have to recognize our sowing and reaping, our seedtime and our harvest. Remember one of the things that the Apostle Paul was doing before God called him to ministry. He was putting Christians in prison. That was a seed and he received a harvest of prison. The bible does not say but maybe God wanted him to plant that seed, because even his prison ministry was successful. He wrote a great deal of the New Testament and some of it while he was in prison.

When you know what seed you have planted and you know that you have been a good steward of your seed you know when the enemy plant things in your ground that you did not plant you can reject it and remind Satan that you did not plant it and you do not have to receive it. Satan knows that but he is hoping that you do not and will receive it anyway in order to plant some future seed. We cannot be complacent when the enemy plants seed. We have to recognize and reject it. Some synonyms for the word steward are agent, overseer, estate manager etc. If we are serious about what we want out of our lives and want to manage our lives better so that we can get the best harvest possible, then we need to plant the right seed.

It all started with God and it all ends with God. Nothing good is coming from anywhere other than from God. He is Alpha and Omega! God is the one that gives us seed. We know this from 2 Corinthians 9:10-12.

*2 Corinthians 9:10-12 Now he that ministereth seed to the sower both minister bread for your food, and multiply your seed sown, and increase the fruits of your righteousness; 11 Being enriched in every thing to all bountifulness, which causeth through us thanksgiving to God. 12 For the administration of this service not only supplieth the want of the saints, but is abundant also by many thanksgivings unto God;*

Here is a final note about the importance of seed. God destroyed the earth with a flood because of bad seed, which means He hates bad seed. The report of this is found in Genesis 6:1-7.

*Genesis 6:1-7 And it came to pass, when men began to multiply on the face of the earth, and daughters were born unto them, 2 That the sons of God saw the daughters of men that they were fair; and they took them wives of all which they chose. 3 And the LORD said, My spirit shall not always strive with man, for that he also is flesh: yet his days shall be an hundred and twenty years. 4 There were giants in the earth in those days; and also after that, when the sons of God came in unto the daughters of men, and they bare children to them, the same became mighty men which were of old, men of renown. 5 And*

## THE IMPORTANCE OF SEED

*GOD saw that the wicked- ness of man was great in the earth, and that every imagination of the thoughts of his heart was only evil continually. 6 And it repented the LORD that he had made man on the earth, and it grieved him at his heart. 7 And the LORD said, I will destroy man whom I have created from the face of the earth; both man, and beast, and the creeping thing, and the fowls of the air; for it repenteth me that I have made them.*

We see from this account that the earth was being repopulated with bad seed and God decided to destroy all of the bad seed and start over with Noah. This is significant because our days on the earth in those days were long but now God has limited them to 120 years. After the flood and Noah came from the ark to dry land to repopulate the earth with all of the animals that were in the ark and his family. He built and altar and offered an offering to God, that was a sweet smell to God and the first thing that God said to Noah after that was while the earth remains there will be seedtime and harvest. This is very important because could have said anything to Noah but He talked about seedtime and harvest. The account of this is found in Genesis 8:18-22.

*Genesis 8:18-22 And Noah went forth, and his sons, and his wife, and his sons' wives with him: 19 Every beast, every creeping thing, and every fowl, and whatsoever creepeth upon the earth, after their kinds, went forth out of the ark. 20 And Noah builded an altar unto the LORD; and took of every clean beast, and of every clean fowl, and offered burnt offerings on the altar. 21 And the LORD smelled a sweet savour; and the LORD said in his heart, I will not again curse*

> *the ground any more for man's sake; for the imagination of man's heart is evil from his youth; neither will I again smite any more every thing living, as I have done. 22 While the earth remaineth, seedtime and harvest, and cold and heat, and summer and winter, and day and night shall not cease.*

Notice here that God did not mention spring and fall seasons. He mentions the seasons that are mostly connect with planting seeds and the time of the harvest. You need warm sunlight and water for plants to grow. This is also true of spiritual seed. They need the Holy Spirit that represents the water and Jesus that represents the light. There are only two seasons in Palestine and that is the dry and rainy seasons that equates to summer and winter. You can plant in the dry season but the major time of growth for plants is the rainy season. Remember, the seed needs, ground (soil), water and sun in order to grow. God also mentioned in verse 21 that what was in man's heart, the imagination of man's heart was evil from his youth, and because of that He would not smite every living thing nor curse the ground for man's sake as He had just done. Wow! If we get this our entire life will change forever.

What God is saying is that man will be responsible for his own seasons. Whatever seed he sow will produce a harvest good or bad and neither the ground nor the animals on the planet will ever suffer again because man's bad seed. They have only one seed opportunity and that is a physical seed, but it is man only that has both physical and spiritual seed. God has set up the seasons that are favorable to support sowing and reaping with the seed so that it will all work together for our good if we receive and use only God's seed.

And as long as the earth remains there will be seedtime and harvest. God is the one that gives us seed. His seed will always be good for us. We should not be getting seed from Satan. There are only two sources of seed from Satan or from God there is no in between. The seed of God perpetuates Him and His Glory.

# About The Author

Dr. Cynthia V. White graduated from Ballard Hudson High School in Macon, Georgia. She continued her education at Morris Brown College, Atlanta, Georgia where she received a Bachelor of Science Degree in Mathematics and Education. She has also received a Master of Arts in Biblical Studies, Master of Divinity and a Doctor of Ministry from Maple Springs Baptist Bible College and Seminary, Capitol Heights, Maryland.

Cynthia was employed by the Department of the Navy for 31 years. During her tenure there, she was the head of the following departments: Computer Aided Design and Manufacturing, Industrial Improvement Technologies, Joint Electronic Drawings and Manufacturing of Industrial Data, Military Construction Projects, Service Craft Management and Manufacturing Technology Program Manager for Naval Shipyards. Cynthia is an accomplished conference speaker. She has spoken at the national productivity conferences, naval engineering conferences, research conferences, production conferences and general business conferences.

Cynthia is a strong supporter of community services. She has participated in fund raisers for the March of Dimes and she supports children in need programs. She has been the Chairman of the Board of Directors of the Center for Community Development of Housing for the Mentally Ill and the Aged. She has also been member of the Board of Directors of Bethel House, a community support center for people in need of help and assistance food, housing, education, jobs and other needs.

Currently is a member of Heritage Church International, Waldorf, Maryland where Bishop Rodney S. Walker I serves as Senior Pastor. Under Bishop Walker's leadership and covering, Cynthia serves as the Secretary of Records of the church, Office Manager. She has also served as manager of Kingdom Christian Bookstore. She serves on the staff of Heritage Church International as a Chief Elder, the Overseer of the Apostolic Arm of the ministry and as an Associate Pastor. She has ministered as conference speaker for women, prophetic conferences, financial and business conferences and workshops. She has taught Bible Study at the Department of the Navy under the directions of the Chaplain for the Naval Sea System Command.

Cynthia serves in Bishop R. S. Walker Ministries, where Bishop R. S. Walker is founder and President, as Registrar and head the Registration Department of the School of Prophets and as a Prophetic Presbyter of the ministry. She is an instructor in the Bishop R.S. Walker Ministries Bible College.

Cynthia is the owner and the CEO of her own business. She is accomplished author. She has published three books, Understanding Spiritual Maturity, The Christian Torah and What Your Father Never Told You about Business. She has spoken at several conferences on the subjects of the books. She is preparing to publish the following books: The Power of Seed, The Sycamore Fig Tree – A Living Sacrifice and the Power of the Earth.

www.ingramcontent.com/pod-product-compliance
Lightning Source LLC
Chambersburg PA
CBHW051836090426
42736CB00011B/1834